2006 Poetry Competition for 7-11 year-olds
Young Writers

- Poems For Playtime
Edited by Annabel Cook

Young Writers

First published in Great Britain in 2006 by:
Young Writers
Remus House
Coltsfoot Drive
Peterborough
PE2 9JX
Telephone: 01733 890066
Website: www.youngwriters.co.uk

All Rights Reserved

© Copyright Contributors 2006

SB ISBN 1 84602 606 7

Foreword

Young Writers was established in 1991 and has been passionately devoted to the promotion of reading and writing in children and young adults ever since. The quest continues today. Young Writers remains as committed to the nurturing of poetic and literary talent as ever.

This year's Young Writers competition has proven as vibrant and dynamic as ever and we are delighted to present a showcase of the best poetry from across the UK and in some cases overseas. Each poem has been selected from a wealth of *A Pocketful Of Rhyme* entries before ultimately being published in this, our fourteenth primary school poetry series.

Once again, we have been supremely impressed by the overall quality of the entries we have received. The imagination, energy and creativity which has gone into each young writer's entry made choosing the poems a challenging and often difficult but ultimately hugely rewarding task - the general high standard of the work submitted ensured this opportunity to bring their poetry to a larger appreciative audience.

We sincerely hope you are pleased with this final collection and that you will enjoy *A Pocketful Of Rhyme - Poems For Playtime* for many years to come.

Contents

Bridestowe Primary School, Okehampton
Bethany Seymour (8) — 1
Rachel England (9) — 1

Desford Primary School, Desford
Daniel Holder (11) — 2
Danielle Prime (10) — 2
Jake Ward (11) — 3
Grace Flint (11) — 3
Maria Perkins (10) — 4
Robyn Hughes (10) — 5
Holly Dale (10) — 6
George Marlow (11) — 6

Hawthorns Junior School, Blackburn
Sulaymaan Shaikh (9) — 7
Numan Ahmed (9) — 7
Khadeejah Shaikh (9) — 8
Tunzeen Amarah Mubarak Patel (9) — 8
Mariyah Mahmud (9) — 9
Raeesah Dar (8) — 9
Hawa Badat (9) — 9
Aysha Humayra Abdullah (8) — 10

Kender Primary School, New Cross
Danielle Pope (10) — 10
Fola Solanke (10) — 11
Kieron Campbell (11) — 11
Adama Bangura (10) — 12
Jack Ford (9) — 13
Anita Awanife (10) — 14
Jordan Perrier-Marquis (11) — 14
Zainab Ali (11) — 15
Gabriel McTigue (11) — 15
Priscilla Irenoa (9) — 16
Ricki Abrahams (10) — 16
Coye Hastings (10) — 17
Zainab Yonis (10) — 17

Dino Martin-Pe'er (10)	18
Jason Chuckwu (11)	18
Louie Hackett (10)	18
Jade White (10)	19
Jordan Peters (9)	19
Zachary Major-Moss (11)	20
Callum Duck (10)	20
Michael Ogunyemi (10)	21
Jamel Nelson Iye (11)	21
Farhaanah Ali (11)	21
Melody Adeniran (11)	22
Karim Aabbouz (11)	22
Matthew Clark (11)	23
André Straker Brown (11)	23
Ka Ha (10)	24
Maisie Walker (11)	24
Edna Oppong (11)	25

Macosquin Primary School, Coleraine

Hannah McNeill (9)	25
Corin Cole (9)	26
Jack Davis (9)	26
Robenya Farlow (9)	27
Ruth Adams (9)	27
Lauren Hutchinson (9)	28
Shannon Campbell (9)	28
Chloe Platt (9)	29
Glenn Cole (9)	29
Racheal Lamont (9)	30
Darryl McAleese (8)	30
Kirsty Crawford (10)	31
Christie Tosh (9)	31
Christopher McIntyre (9)	32
Harry Calvin (9)	32
Brad Culbertson (10)	33

Onchan Primary School, Onchan

Becky Turner (11)	33
Annabel Grainger (11)	34
Elizabeth Quayle (11)	35
Laura Cherry (11)	36

Sammie Caine (11)	36
Gemma Granger (11)	37
James Sayle (11)	37
Jessica Duncan (11)	38
Phiranat Khamnok (11)	38
Aalish Foulger (11)	39
Kieran Moore (11)	39
Lily Purdy (11)	40
Lorna Griffiths (11)	40
Laura Atkinson (11)	41
Ryan Jones (11)	42

Padfield Community Primary School, Padfield

Megan McMylor (11)	42
Cameron Neve (11)	43

Poyntzpass Primary School, Newry

Shannon Hazlett (10)	43
Jacob Cairns (10)	43
Emma Liggett (11)	44
James Thompson (10)	44
Matthew Patterson (11)	44
Ashley Morrow (10)	45
Matthew Denny (11)	45
Robbie Clarke (11)	45
Jillian Wilson (10)	46
Chelsea Ellison (10)	46
Christopher Smart (9)	47
Judith Alderdice (10)	47
Ryan McClure (10)	48
Ross McMullan (10)	48
Russell Graham (10)	48
Richard Corry (10)	49

St John's CE Primary School, Burscough

Ben Lawrence (8)	49
Ryan Byrne (8)	49
Emma Leary (9)	49
Joshua Birchall (9)	50
Ellie Gorton (9)	50
Jack Winders (9)	50

Andrew Hawick (9)	51
Tara Davies (8)	51
Charlotte Booth (8)	51
Hayley Medlock (9)	52
Sarah Baker (9)	52

Thongsley Fields Primary & Nursery School, Huntingdon

Stephen French (9)	52
Lauren Whitham (9)	53
Aisha Russell (8)	53
Jack James (9)	53
Carwyn Kelly (9)	54
Melissa Seymour (9)	54

West Jesmond Primary School, Newcastle upon Tyne

Shaun Beardsley (9)	54
William Haigh (9)	55
Aya Hegab (10)	55
Jonah Vinsome (10)	56
Horia Dragoi (9)	56
Charles Antons (10)	57
Lydia Reeve (9)	57
Ruairidh Chester (9)	58
Zulekha Sadiq (10)	58
Aisha Omer-Hellings (10)	59
Robert Kreibich (9)	59
Molly O'Brien (10)	60
Emily Armitage (10)	61
Rayyan Qureshi (10)	61
Sophie Neibig (10)	62
Ella Davenport (9)	62
Valeria Laird (10)	63
Gaby Knops (10)	63
Rachel Jacques (9)	64
Lucy Dinsdale (9)	64
David Goodwin (9)	65
Max Parker (10)	65
William Green (9)	66
Berina Stitkovac (10)	66
Raz Gharbi (10)	67
Adam O'Mara (10)	67

Rachel Laidler (10)	68
Henry Winter (9)	68
Emma Sin Yee Lip (10)	69
Saman Karimi (9)	69
Matthew Moore (10)	70
Gerry Rowland (9)	70
Sophie Barker (10)	71
Elliott Dixon (9)	71
Yasmina Carlton (10)	72
Jamie Meikle (10)	72
Hattie Airey (10)	73
Aaliyah Khan (10)	73
Chloe Wilson (10)	74
Zoe Hovells (10)	74
Tamandeep Singh Lally (9)	75
Jessica Peach (9)	75
Becky Franks (9)	76
Ahmed Bouchelouche (10)	76
Waleed Saqib (9)	77
Joe Blair (10)	78
Lucy Chappel (9)	78
Haris Ghani (10)	78
Liberty Smart (9)	79
Chloe McClements (9)	79
Liam Green (10)	80
Simon Grabham (10)	80
Sam Thompson (10)	81

West Twyford Primary School, Park Royal

Ali Osman (7)	81
Monica Edwards (7)	81
Zahrah Islam (7)	82
Shanika Smith (8)	82
Diadean Wazait (8)	82
Kyle Peters-Liverpool (8)	83
Toni Ribezzo (8)	83
Zainab Lawi (8)	83
Erion Xhixha (9)	84
Anushka Sabapara (8)	84
Crystal Toppin (9)	84
Adham Chakhachiro (9)	85

Toby Yong (9)	85
Kai Butcher (8)	85
Rayeen Rahman (9)	86
Haoyang Xu (9)	86
Owais Khan (9)	87
Matthew Butcher (9)	87
Daniel Mooney (8)	88
Rika Ramesh (8)	88
Alexia Ryan (9)	88
Lucy O'Driscoll (10)	89
Sebri Addous (9)	89
Julia Parissien (10)	90
Siobhan Abrams-Brand (10)	90
Kais Al-Kaisi (9)	90
Rebecca Cheung (9)	91
Michaela Devaughan (8)	91
Jade Cassin (8)	91
Yianick Green-Morrison (10)	92
Ali Joseph (8)	92
Sean Hatoum (8)	93
Mitchell Gardner (7)	93
Faith Allen (8)	93
Jessica Livingstone (10)	94
Natalia Sieczkarek (10)	94
Manita Gujral (9)	95
Maham Sajjad	95
Summayyah Khan (8)	95
Anjali Karadia (10)	96
Rut Patel (10)	96
Robert Graham (9)	97
Mennat Soliman (10)	97
Daniel Doroodvash (9)	97
Tania Rull (10)	98
Zed Asassa (10)	98

Withnell Fold Primary School, Chorley

Matthew Critchley (9)	98
Lucy Turnock (10)	99
Fionach Miller (10)	99
Megan Davis (10)	100
Kate Widdowson (11)	101

Anna Hopkin (10)	102
Thomas Radziminski (9)	102
Rocky Widdowson (9)	103
Harriet Tallon (11)	103
Ali Wrigley (11)	104
Joshua Jackson (11)	105
Carla Davy (11)	106
Greg Smith (10)	107
Sophie Parry (10)	108
Lewis Gabbott (10)	109
Daniel Lane (11)	109
Luke McCarrick (10)	110
Natasha McMahon (11)	111
Bethany Wood (11)	112
Sam Fenton (9)	113
Alice Sofield (9)	114
Sam Cartwright (10)	115

The Poems

A Sad Tale

Little Miss Bake
Sat by the lake
Eating her blackberry pie
Along came a fish
Who swallowed the dish
And took the blackberry pie

Little Miss Bake
Had tummy ache
Because the fish was so sly
The fish gave a wave
And said he'd behave
Let's hope this isn't a lie!

Bethany Seymour (8)
Bridestowe Primary School, Okehampton

Circles Of Love

Huge rings, teeny rings
Pretty, sparkly, precious things
Rings for weddings
Last forever
They adorn a lady's finger
Friends give rings to show their loving
Rings show happiness
Rings jingle and tingle
Rings can fit on the tiniest finger
Rings for your ears, not just your hands
Gorgeous jewels set in gold
Shining diamonds set in silver
Sometimes they get lost in the sand
But the rings' circle of love goes on forever.

Rachel England (9)
Bridestowe Primary School, Okehampton

Sun - Haikus

Searing glowing orb
Shooting massive orange flames
Essential to life

Not to be looked at
The brightest star we can see
Dead at even-fall

Hangs in dark mid-space
Orbits the dark universe
Spins on its axis.

Daniel Holder (11)
Desford Primary School, Desford

It's Not Fair!

It's not fair, I can't have a pet dog,
Hog or frog!
I can't have a pet cat,
Rat or even a bat!
I can't have a gorilla
Or even a little chinchilla!
I can't have a pet bee
Or even a tiny flea!
I want a pet whale
Or maybe a little snail,
I've asked my parents for all of these things,
But secretly I don't mind
For I have a secret pet elephant
At the bottom of my garden!

Danielle Prime (10)
Desford Primary School, Desford

TV Has Ruined My Imagination!

TV is a bomb,
Destroying my imagination,
TV is a Hoover,
Sucking up my imagination,
Wrecking my brain . . .

This glowing picture,
Shimmers in the dark,
TV tears people apart,
Like Velcro,
Draining my life . . .

TV is like cigarettes,
Addictive but harmful,
It's a monster,
Unstoppable,
Melting my mind . . .

TV is slowly killing me,
Turning my blood sour,
Destroying my reflexes,
Wrecking my senses,
Destroying my imagination . . .

Jake Ward (11)
Desford Primary School, Desford

Fairies

Pixies here - brownies there, twirling amongst the mist
That towering castle, tall and proud, is home to loving risks
The falling of a fairy, results in non-belief
For twining around the gardens, is never-locking grief
Faithful hearts of stolen twilight dust
The lush mint grass, coated in a diamond crust
Enchanting woodlands are bathed in rosy light from the sunset
And when the day turns the frosty stars illuminate any threat.

Grace Flint (11)
Desford Primary School, Desford

Seasons

Summer is a heatwave of joy and laughter
Summer is when the flowers are in full bloom
Summer is a time for sunbathing, garden parties
And days out at the park
Summer is when the sun sizzles like a red balloon
Floating in the pink sky
Summer is the time when rivers dry out and droughts occur
Summer is the warmest season of them all
Summer is the daisy chain time of year
You will know when summer is here.

Spring is a happy time of year
When newborn lambs take their first steps to freedom
And see the first blossom fall at their feet
When the daffodils paint the fields with their bright colours
The whole world is a colourful globe
Waiting to explode in a palette of colours.

Autumn is when the crispy leaves swamp the floor
And the trees are all bare
A whirlwind of leaves surrounds you
Until the gust of wind dies down
And the sound of leaves crunching beneath your feet
Is like the rustling of an old newspaper.

Winter is when icicles hang from window ledges
Winter is when snowmen stand in every front garden of every house
Winter is when fields stand coated in snow-white sugar
Winter is when newborn babies see the first snowflakes
Fall through the air.

Maria Perkins (10)
Desford Primary School, Desford

Here In Food City

Houses out of chocolate cake,
The school a huge chunk of cheese,
Rivers into a sugar lake,
Trees as candy canes giving off a breeze,
Here in Food City.

Roads out of strawberry icing,
The cars blocks of toffee,
Big Ben into an onion ring
And wet puddles of coffee,
Here in Food City.

People out of marshmallows,
Buildings out of chips,
The sea into milk that flows,
It tingles when it touches my lips,
Here in Food City.

Pencils out of French fries,
Paper, slices of toast,
Everyone loves it, especially the flies
And TV's a pork roast,
Here in Food City.

As I silently get into bed,
I even dream of food,
Monsters with jelly eyes flashing red,
Creating a scary feast-filled mood,
Here in Food City.

Robyn Hughes (10)
Desford Primary School, Desford

Favourite Words

Sea anemone, skedaddle, thwack, spook,
Not forgetting gobbledegook,
Banana, whisper, queasy, squirm,
Words that wiggle like a worm,
Doodah, whatsit, widget and thingy,
Bouncy, daring, audacious and springy.

These are words that make you feel nice,
Giggly, higgledy, sugar and spice,
Circle, shape and fancy squiggle,
Bubbly, cuddly, wriggly, wiggle,
Tongue-twisting words that roll off the tongue,
Read them, write them, sing as a song.

Soft, squidgy, flumpety, squish,
Salty, wrinkly, old smelly fish,
Fluffy, fuzzy, buzzy bee,
Where words come from is a mystery,
These words bring us pleasure and glee,
Words are essential for you and me.

Holly Dale (10)
Desford Primary School, Desford

The Soul Of Music

The mesmerising vocals that shiver your spine
The drums as a heartbeat thrill your mind
Rhythms never seem to break away
They could carry on playing for the rest of the day
The lyrics keep on going, they find it hard to stop
You have the rock, pop and the great hip-hop
But it's not the sound of the voice in your head
It carries on singing till you're comfy in bed
Then you switch on your stereo, track number 10
And the musical rhythm starts over again.

George Marlow (11)
Desford Primary School, Desford

Our Magic Chest
(Based on 'Magic Box' by Kit Wright)

We are putting in our chest . . .
The humming sound of the computer
The noise of the elevator
The scraping noise of the scraper.

We are putting in our chest . . .
The ringing of the phone
The shouting in the soccer dome
The sound of the doorbell pressed when coming home.

Our chest is made of . . .
The colours of the rainbow
The ice of comets
The clear ocean floor
And four different phones.

We will . . .
Travel through time in the chest
And store our secrets
Contact our friends all the time
Play games
And get wishes granted.

Sulaymaan Shaikh (9)
Hawthorns Junior School, Blackburn

Art

Art is my favourite thing
I think I'm the artist king
I like to draw
I love to put on a show
One day I'll have my name in lights
It will be so bright
I know!

Numan Ahmed (9)
Hawthorns Junior School, Blackburn

My Brother

My brother is very vicious
And is always unconscious,
He doesn't have a sense of humour
And is certainly not miraculous,
The reason is obvious,
He is not fabulous,
He is a science maniac,
He is fast and furious,
He is not oblivious,
He is totally ridiculous,
People say he is dangerous,
He will send you round and round the bend,
Because he mischievous,
Lots of people say he is mysterious,
He is known as notorious,
For always being spontaneous,
There is only one thing left to say,
He is a total genius!

Khadeejah Shaikh (9)
Hawthorns Junior School, Blackburn

The Best

H awthorns are the greatest
A ll the children are well behaved
W e work as a team
T eachers are always there for us
H appy and proud kids
O ther children want to come here
R ackets are not heard
N o one fights
S ensible, sweet, super children!

Tunzeen Amarah Mubarak Patel (9)
Hawthorns Junior School, Blackburn

Family

F abulous and love to hide
A lways by my side
M y wonderful family
I mportant and help happily
L oving and caring
Y es! We love sharing!

Mariyah Mahmud (9)
Hawthorns Junior School, Blackburn

Friends

F orever friends together
R eally, really nice
I ntelligent and kind
E specially helpful
N early always there for me
D on't break up when things get bad
S o don't be lonely and despair!

Raeesah Dar (8)
Hawthorns Junior School, Blackburn

The Golden Star

Brightly shining above the sky
Glittering like a thousand eyes
Beautifully lit like candlelight
Taking me on a wonderful flight
I live upon the sun and moon
Twinkling like a shining spoon.

Hawa Badat (9)
Hawthorns Junior School, Blackburn

Seasons

S ummer, autumn, winter, spring
E vergreen trees nice to see
A utumn when the leaves become brown
S ummer with butterflies and bees
O ver the meadows, hills and trees
N ice and cool in the shady light
S ummer's gone now, it's time for autumn to come.

Aysha Humayra Abdullah (8)
Hawthorns Junior School, Blackburn

The Songs Of Lucy, Aslan, Edmund And Susan
(Inspired by 'The Lion, The Witch And The Wardrobe' by C S Lewis)

It's called love!
Peter, Susan, Edmund
My brothers and sister
Even though Edmund betrayed me
I still love him.

It's called power!
Even though I know
I have power over the witch
I still want to defeat her
She has no power over me.

It's called jealousy!
I am not jealous
It's just what they think
If their attitude doesn't change
I'll get the queen to turn them into stone.

It's called forgiveness!
Should we forgive him
Or shouldn't we forgive him?
He betrayed Lucy and has been ghastly
But I still forgive him.

Danielle Pope (10)
Kender Primary School, New Cross

Train Journey

I was rushing to the train station
Getting breakfast on the way
Choo, choo, choo
Finally on the train eating breakfast
And playing different kinds of games
Choo, choo, choo, choo, choo
We are now moving and I can see houses, gardens and parks
There are many things to see
Choo, choo, choo, choo, choo, choo
I have now had a nap and many hours have now gone
Also I am getting bored of all the pleasant games
Choo, choo, choo, choo, choo, choo, choo
I can now see the crystal-blue ocean leading out very far
Until the sky meets the sea, which is very far out if you think about it
Choo, choo, choo, choo, choo, choo, choo, choo, choo
We are now going through a jade-green forest
Hip hip hooray, we are now in the country town
I can see houses and other things, also big and large buildings
Choo, choo, choo, choo, choo, choo, choo, choo, choo
We are now in the station, see you on my way back
Goodbye!

Fola Solanke (10)
Kender Primary School, New Cross

The Park

The park is somewhere you can find a lot of friends,
Willing to hold your hand
Or cover your back
Whenever necessary.

The park is where you can feel as safe as a cub
Being guarded by its caring parents.

The park smells like the wind
Viciously ripping and tearing
Through the bright, green grass.

Kieron Campbell (11)
Kender Primary School, New Cross

My Journey To School

I walk outside
I feel chilly
And smell the scent of toast
I see the squirrels scatter
In the cold and have some fun
The winter's cold.
I see orange
Brick-brown and black
And hear parents
Telling off their
Cheeky children
And laughing
At the mischief
While I have no one
Beside me
I feel lonely
And cold!
I stroll and hear my fruit
Smashing together
In my bag
While I run
For nothing
And the smash
Gets louder
And quieter
I run into the door
Like a new adventure
I see different people
And sometimes
It's like my life
Repeated again
I then hear
A noise
That goes *ding-dong*
The bell continues
Then a stampede
Of elephants
Is my life over?

Adama Bangura (10)
Kender Primary School, New Cross

My Journey To The London Aquarium

The bus
Was crowded
And loud
It smelt of
Diesel
I got off
The bus
And I approached
The aquarium
It was enormous
It was blue and black
When I trotted in
It was gigantic
In there, the tanks were huge
The sharks were massive
The fish were small
The manta rays were big
The pressure was big on the glass
When I went
Into the next room
I saw a round, glass table
When I looked over
There were manta rays
You were allowed
To touch them
I touched a small manta ray
It fell like sandpaper
But underneath
It is soft and smooth
The big manta rays
Stayed at the bottom
The water was freezing
I could hardly touch the water
The little manta rays
Liked being touched
They loved being touched
They absolutely loved it!

Jack Ford (9)
Kender Primary School, New Cross

My Journey To School

I can smell
The freshness
Of the early morning breeze
And a start of a new day
In the summer
The scent of the beautiful
Blossoming flowers
As I pass people's delightful gardens
I can see many colours
All the colours of the rainbow
My feet touch the rigid concrete
Sometimes, if I listen closely
I can hear the trees swaying
And I can hear children playing.

Anita Awanife (10)
Kender Primary School, New Cross

Adventure Playground

An adventure playground can be fun
But it can be disrespectful
Smells like a rotten apple exploding on you
Tastes like salt and vinegar dissolving in your mouth.

An adventure playground can be fun
But it can be disrespectful
To play the pool table is long and wide
But you need to be over five
You might even want to skive
To go to an adventure playground
An adventure playground can be fun
But it can be disrespectful.

Jordan Perrier-Marquis (11)
Kender Primary School, New Cross

London

London is a legendary place for a memorable tour
London is a place nobody will bore.

London sounds like a silent giggle
London is the colour blue when a baby is born
London is a legendary place.

London is a legendary place
For an unforgettable tour
London is a place nobody will bore.

London has a tranquil, contrasting air
London is a place nobody can ignore
London is a mini adventure world.

London is a legendary place
For a memorable tour
London is a place nobody will bore.

London is an international city
London is forever the best place
London is a place you can't live without.

London is a legendary place
For an unforgettable tour
London is a place nobody will bore.

London.

Zainab Ali (11)
Kender Primary School, New Cross

London

The smell of the bus,
Stuffy people not knowing where to go,
This is London, still amazing.

Gabriel McTigue (11)
Kender Primary School, New Cross

The Charming Angels
(Inspired by 'The Rime of the Ancient Mariner' by Samuel Taylor Coleridge)

A glamorous light,
Liking a shining halo on an angel's head.
As gold as the sea water,
As warm as the sea.

As grey as a wind fog,
As the windy fog lies in the mist.
As scary as a ghostly ship,
As it goes slowly through the sea.

As bright as light shining down
From Heaven on the ghostly ship.
As if angels were haunting it like a haunted house.

As a large army of angels going up
To Heaven to tell their master
They've won the battle.

Priscilla Irenoa (9)
Kender Primary School, New Cross

The Death Of The Albatross
(Inspired by 'The Rime of the Ancient Mariner' by Samuel Taylor Coleridge)

The sharp arrow shot swiftly through the air
The needle-sharp bow brought darkness
Towards the albatross as it glided down.

Just say, just say dead nor darker nor dimmer
The sight of the day could have been
The icebergs sharp and icier than could be
The speed to kill in a monster's way.

Oh, why, oh why, oh mighty, nor light just dark
In darkness and death on his way, nor one word to say
Dead as dead could be, the albatross laid upon me.

Ricki Abrahams (10)
Kender Primary School, New Cross

The Rime Of The Ancient Mariner
(Inspired by 'The Rime of the Ancient Mariner' by Samuel Taylor Coleridge)

The piercing arrow like killing it prey

Like the albatross cutting a good smile and dies at the dead end.

Like the Devil sent an arrow to kill the good
Lord of the sky and the bird who blew the
Wind, the one who made wind go.

It is just like life has gone down
The dirty drain.

It is like a devil's soul arrow going
Starting to go, go at the target at the back of

An albatross' heart.

Coye Hastings (10)
Kender Primary School, New Cross

The Rainbow's Powers
(Inspired by 'The Rime of the Ancient Mariner' by Samuel Taylor Coleridge)

Like fire trying to break through water,
The rainbow splits the sky.
Like strong perfume drawing you forward,
The rainbow hustles the clouds up high.

Like water trying to break through fire,
The rainbow sparkles down low.
Like strong perfume drawing you forward,
The rainbow thrusts to show the reminding of the bow.

Like water and fire having a battle,
The rainbow's like a rope in a tug of war.
Like strong perfume drawing you forward,
The rainbow was the key of law.

Zainab Yonis (10)
Kender Primary School, New Cross

The Stare Of Death
(Inspired by 'The Rime of the Ancient Mariner' by Samuel Taylor Coleridge)

The cloak as dark as the night sky
When the stars are hidden
Mouldy bones like a pale, dead body,
Golden locks like sand flowing through the air,
The ripped sails trailing down.

The mast dropped down
And Death stayed still
No fear in his face
Nor any liveliness.

Dino Martin-Pe'er (10)
Kender Primary School, New Cross

Happiness

Happiness tastes like delicious food
Happiness is blue like a cloudless sky
Happiness sounds like birds singing
Happiness reminds me of playing football
Happiness looks like people being kind
Happiness feels like sunshine
Happiness smells like chips!

Jason Chuckwu (11)
Kender Primary School, New Cross

Death
(Inspired by 'The Rime of the Ancient Mariner' by Samuel Taylor Coleridge)

Ship as Hell sucks your blood from your eye
Now twilight within the courts of the sun
Man's blood runs with cold
Sky as white as a human pale face
Hollow eyes like dark, deep holes.

Louie Hackett (10)
Kender Primary School, New Cross

The Sun, The Sea And The Darkness
(Based on 'The Rime of the Ancient Mariner' by Samuel Taylor Coleridge)

The sun now rose upon the right,
Darkness was appearing.
The albatross is dead,
Nobody was cheering.

Who had killed him?
Why had they?
He's dead, he's dead,
I heard a sailor say.

His blood was in the sea,
It looked like a slithering snake,
He looked cold,
He was beginning to shake.

Oh no, oh no, what have I done?
The ancient mariner said.
Has his men seen it?
He watched the albatross dead.

Jade White (10)
Kender Primary School, New Cross

The Rime Of The Ancient Mariner
(Based on 'The Rime of the Ancient Mariner' by Samuel Taylor Coleridge)

Rushing from the bleeding Hell as fire in the ocean,
The fair breeze blew, the white foam flew,
As it pushed the wind, it grew and grew.

Misty fog, steam blazing across your pathway
From the demon ocean, reel and rout,
Kill and shout in the killing sea.

Red as blood through the flushing water,
Splash and bash, spill and kill,
Blushing and crushing in the blood glooming water.

The sea is flushing with cold-blooded spirits
From under the Hell funk was all over the bloody water.

Jordan Peters (9)
Kender Primary School, New Cross

London

I see squalid streets
Dreary water, smoky days
In blaring London.

Where the heart of England is
It can be deep and wonderful
Wonderful and deep
Where the heart of England is

London is endless
It is like the circle of life
In blaring London

Where the heart of England is
It can be deep and wonderful
Wonderful and deep
Where the heart of England is

Beautiful buildings
Are destroyed by hideous
Streets, what is London?

Zachary Major-Moss (11)
Kender Primary School, New Cross

Angels
(Inspired by 'The Rime of the Ancient Mariner' by Samuel Taylor Coleridge)

An angel leaning on another
Looking down at the dead, rotting bodies
Beautiful angels floating above the salty Dead Sea
The dead bodies lay peacefully
And one man, alive
Just crawling, lonely, half-dead
Just like in Hell
The men, dried and wrinkled
The man looking up at the group of pretty angels.

Callum Duck (10)
Kender Primary School, New Cross

Hunger

Hunger sounds like a drum beating
Hunger reminds me of darkness
Hunger feels like a rugged surface
Hunger smells like thin air
Hunger tastes like a disintegrating rat
Hunger is like a black hole
Hunger looks like a brown leaf falling from the branch.

Michael Ogunyemi (10)
Kender Primary School, New Cross

Fear

Fear reminds me of the dark, inky sky
Because the darkness is as deep as outer space
Fear sounds like a huge bear about to eat me
Fear feels mouldy and repulsive
Fear smells like a baby's dirty nappy
Fear tastes like an old smelly boot, as nasty as a sweaty shirt
Fear is dark blue like the ocean.

Jamel Nelson Iye (11)
Kender Primary School, New Cross

Emptiness

Emptiness looks like the landscape after a nuclear war
Emptiness smells like the air after a summer storm
Emptiness feels like the deepest, saddest pit of depression
Emptiness sounds like a hollow cavern echoing in the distance
Emptiness tastes like hunger, a cub prowling for food
Emptiness reminds me of an empty, dark corner
Emptiness is the colour of a dull, colourless sky.

Farhaanah Ali (11)
Kender Primary School, New Cross

My Street

Quiet, little street
Bang, crash, dom!
I was wrong
Noisy neighbours
Mad music
Thudding trainers.

Big, spacious street
Brom, whack, drap!
I was wrong
Careless cars
Malicious motorbikes
Ferocious vans.

Fun, playful street
Whoosh, zip, drip!
I was wrong
Terrible thunder
Ravenous rain
Lustful lightning.

Things aren't always as they seem.

Melody Adeniran (11)
Kender Primary School, New Cross

My House

My house is tall like the Statue of Liberty
My house is as white as the White House
My house is too big for King Kong to climb up
My house smells like an air freshener
My house is so big, I could put 900 footballs inside
My house has a cellar with 16 elephants in it
My house is secure like an army building
My house is guarded with 56 guard dogs.

Karim Aabbouz (11)
Kender Primary School, New Cross

House

My house is dynamic!
It is a fun house
It smells like roses blowing in the summer wind
It looks like a beautiful mansion filled with love

My house is dynamic!
It is a fun house
It is huge like a castle
It is exciting

My house is dynamic!
It is a fun house
It is packed sometimes but not always
It feels like being in a warm, safe place

My house is dynamic
It is a fun house
The TV is fun, sometimes entertaining
It is loud, sometimes booming

My house is dynamic!
It is a funhouse
It is a thrilling place of adventure
It is an exciting place

My house is dynamic!
It is a fun house.

Matthew Clark (11)
Kender Primary School, New Cross

Calm

Calm looks like the wide space of a football pitch
Calm sounds like the smooth, mellow sounds of classical music
Calm smells like the fresh smell of a new Mercedes
Calm reminds me of the gentle cold breeze on your neck
And the bright blue sky that puts you to sleep in the afternoon
Calm tastes like the wide blue sea.

André Straker Brown (11)
Kender Primary School, New Cross

The Haunted House

It sounds like a fierce scream from an eagle,
The impure blood living off a soul's flesh.
It smells like the freshly burnt lava erupting
And the elongated death - forever.
The house haunts me, for evermore,
The wind is gripping me like a hand,
I need help, but cannot speak out
And the elongated death - forever.
All the scents of death suffocate you
Until your strength has gone,
Like a creature lost in a deadly, dark world,
Like a flashback that is always there in front of me
And the elongated death - forever.

Ka Ha (10)
Kender Primary School, New Cross

Fear

Fear is the colour of nothing, a hollow cavern yearning for attention
Fear looks like a black cat prowling the land for its latest catch
Fear sounds like the ticking of a bomb
Waiting greedily for an unexpected guest
Fear smells like fire surrounding you
Everlasting and ever stronger
Fear tastes like a drop of bitter lemon encasing your throat in Hell
Fear feels like sandpaper grating your skin into shreds
Of woe and misery
Fear reminds me of the night placing its veil of deadly destruction
over you
Destroying all hope
Fear is death itself.

Maisie Walker (11)
Kender Primary School, New Cross

Darkness

Darkness is black like my empty soul
Darkness reminds me of a half-moon in a forest
Darkness sounds like a whisper of a ghost
Darkness smells like fresh blood from a vampire's soup
Darkness feels like a dead, haunted mansion
Darkness tastes like a sour, poisoned apple
Darkness, darkness, darkness!

Edna Oppong (11)
Kender Primary School, New Cross

What Is Pink?

Pink is the colour of ballet shoes
Pink is the colour of a ribbon in your hair
Pink is the colour of butterflies floating in the air
Pink is the colour of a woolly jumper
Pink is the colour of strawberry milkshake
Pink is the colour of your favourite party frock
Pink is the sound of a baby breathing
Pink is the sound of ballet music
Pink is the sound of whispering
Pink makes me feel so happy
Pink makes me feel relaxed
Pink is the colour of my gloves
Pink is the colour of my socks
Pink is the colour of pretty summer flowers
Pink is the sound of birds singing
Pink is my favourite colour.

Hannah McNeill (9)
Macosquin Primary School, Coleraine

What Is White?

White is snow falling in winter
White is clean, clear paper
White is a hairband to put up my hair
White is a rubber that I use to rub out with
White is a flower that you can smell
White is a wristband you wear around your wrist
White is a paper bag to put things in
White is a clock that goes *tick, tock, tick*
White is a polar bear that growls
White is a wedding car carrying a bride
White is the phone my teacher uses in school
White is fluffy clouds up in the sky
White is houses in a field
White is a shirt your dad wears to work
White is silence all around
White is a girl who sings so low
White is a baby breathing
White is a violin playing
White is a flute's note
White makes you relax
White makes you tired all day long
That's what makes white white.

Corin Cole (9)
Macosquin Primary School, Coleraine

What Is Blue?

Blue is the colour of a fast racing car
Blue is the colour of the sky
Blue is when someone cries
Blue is my school T-shirt
Blue is a cuddly, woolly jumper
Blue is my heavy schoolbag
Blue is the colour of my class curtains
Blue is the colour of frosty winter mornings
I love blue.

Jack Davis (9)
Macosquin Primary School, Coleraine

What Is Green?

Green is the colour of long, wavy grass growing taller
Green is the colour of a shiny fish swimming in the pond
Green is the colour of my favourite T-shirt I wear
Green is the colour of a book my sister reads
Green is the colour of my sister's eyes
Green is the colour of my hairband
Green is the colour of a jelly frog jumping around the place
Green is the colour of fresh leaves falling from the trees
Green is the colour of my tights
Green is the colour of our classroom door
Green is the colour of a Celtic top
Green is the colour of curtains
Green is the peas we eat for tea
Green is the long dress my mum wears
Green is unripe bananas
I love green.

Robenya Farlow (9)
Macosquin Primary School, Coleraine

What Is Blue?

Blue is the colour of the sky
Blue is the colour of bluebells in the meadow
Blue is the colour of the water that splashes over rocks
Blue is the colour of a paper towel
Blue is the sound of water running over stone
Blue is the sound of ice melting on the snow
Blue is the sound of snowflakes falling
Blue is the sound of people crying
Blue is the colour that makes me feel sad
Blue makes me feel lonely when I can't join in the games
Blue makes me feel unhappy when it is raining
I love blue.

Ruth Adams (9)
Macosquin Primary School, Coleraine

What Is Yellow?

Yellow is sunshine that shines in the sky
Yellow is the colour of ducks splashing in the pond
Yellow is the colour of a sunflower growing tall
Yellow is the colour of a daffodil's face
Yellow is shoes that are nice and shiny
Yellow is the sound of a pair of earrings rattling
Yellow is the sound of curtains blowing in the wind
Yellow is the sound of a pencil rolling on the desk
Yellow is the sound of a bed creaking
Yellow is the sound of chicks pecking on the ground
Yellow is feeling happy
Yellow is feeling enjoyable
Yellow is feeling bright
I love yellow.

Lauren Hutchinson (9)
Macosquin Primary School, Coleraine

What Is Pink?

Pink is the colour of candyfloss which I like to eat
Pink is the colour of my pencil case where I keep my pencils
Pink is the colour of a Slush Puppy
Pink is the colour of my duvet
Pink is the colour of my ink pen
Pink is the colour of my mum's bag
Pink makes me feel happy
Pink is my pretty bedroom
Pink is the gentle sound of a baby breathing
Pink is the colour of pretty flowers in the garden
Pink is the colour of my good shoes
Pink is the colour of my skirt which I like to wear
Pink is my favourite colour.

Shannon Campbell (9)
Macosquin Primary School, Coleraine

What Is Blue?

Blue is the colour of the sky which birds fly through
Blue is the colour of the sea where fish live
Blue is the colour of a big rubber ball that rolls around the street
Blue is the colour of a sports car which I would love to drive all day
Blue is the colour of my jumper I wear to school
Blue is the colour of my dad's car
Blue is the carpet on my bedroom floor
Blue is the colour of a Slush Puppy I like
Blue is the colour of my eyes
Blue is the colour of my new ink pen I use in school
Blue makes me feel sad when I can't join in a game
Blue makes me feel so relaxed
Blue sometimes makes me feel upset
When I have no one to play with
Blue is the sound of a baby crying
Blue is the sound of paper towels being scrunched up
Blue is the colour of my maths book
I love blue.

Chloe Platt (9)
Macosquin Primary School, Coleraine

What Is Blue?

Blue is the colour of a car
Blue makes me feel relaxed
Blue is the sound of the sea splashing upon the rocks
Blue is the colour of my schoolbag
Blue is the colour of my school jumper
Blue is the colour of my English book
Blue is the colour of the minibus
Blue is the colour of the sky
And blue is the colour of rushing water.

Glenn Cole (9)
Macosquin Primary School, Coleraine

What Is Blue?

Blue is the colour of my auntie's car which speeds along
Blue is the sound of the wind blowing through trees in wintertime
Blue makes me feel unhappy because it's cold
Blue is the summer sky that I lie under and look up at
Blue is the sky that fluffy clouds float in
Blue is the sound of the sea that crashes against rocks
Blue is the colour of balloons I like
Blue is the colour of bluebells in a summer meadow
Blue is feeling tired
Blue is the colour of our clipboards in school
I love blue!

Racheal Lamont (9)
Macosquin Primary School, Coleraine

What Is Blue?

Blue is the colour of the sky which birds fly through
Blue is the colour of the sea where hungry sharks live
Blue is the colour of a ball which bounces along the street
Blue is my jumper that I wear to school
Blue is the colour of the floor that we all walk on
Blue is the sound of water trickling down the stream
Blue is ink that I write with
Blue is the feeling of sadness that everyone gets sometimes
Blue is the sound of hailstones tapping on my window
Blue is the sound of rain that hits my umbrella
Blue is the sound of my mum's washing machine
Blue is a special colour
A colour that I adore
Blue is a wonderful colour.

Darryl McAleese (8)
Macosquin Primary School, Coleraine

What Is Green?

Green is a lovely colour
I love with all my heart
Green is the colour that makes me feel happy, really happy
Green is the colour of the grass when the wind blows
Green is the colour my ink pen used to be
Green is the colour of the sea splashing against the rocks
Green is the colour of the trees rocking from side to side
Green is a baby breathing heavily
Green is the sound of a bird tweeting in the morning
Green is the colour of our classroom in the school
Green is the colour that makes me content
Green is the colour of the paint in B&Q.

Kirsty Crawford (10)
Macosquin Primary School, Coleraine

What Is Blue?

Blue is the colour of diamonds sparkling in the light
Blue is the sign of sadness when you watch sad movies
Blue is the sound when you are walking on crunchy snow
Blue is the colour of a car speeding past
Blue is the colour of blueberries dangling from the trees
Blue is the sound of a baby crying
Blue is the feeling of loneliness when you have no friends
Blue is the sound of snowflakes falling
I love blue!

Christie Tosh (9)
Macosquin Primary School, Coleraine

What Is Black?

Black is a pen that I write with in school
Black is a can of Coke that fizzes when I shake it
Black is a sports car speeding along the road
Black is a forest, deep and scary
Black is a band playing very loud music
Black is sunglasses that I wear in summer
Black is the shoes that I wear to school
Black is a piece of chocolate cake
Black is the chair that Miss Taylor has in class
Black is a rock band
Black is a sports car
Black is the squeaking of a pen on a board
Black is thunder and lightning
Black is the silence of a dark room
Black is the bang of a bomb
Black is the squeaking of a dark forest
Black is the squeaking of a door
Black is the scream of a woman
Black is the sound of a dog
Black is a scary sound
Black is the colour of ink
Black makes you think of revenge
Black is the colour of my cousin's dog
I love black.

Christopher McIntyre (9)
Macosquin Primary School, Coleraine

What Is Blue?

Blue is the sky on a summer's day
Blue is a fast racing car
Blue is the sound of a baby crying
Blue makes me feel happy
Blue is the balloon floating high in the air
Blue is the sparkling water of the sea.

Harry Calvin (9)
Macosquin Primary School, Coleraine

What Is Blue?

Blue is the colour of the sea on a sunny day
Blue is the colour of a car
Blue is the colour of my school jumper
Blue is the colour of my eyes
Blue is a cold colour
Blue is the colour for boys to wear
Blue is the colour of a drink
Blue is sometimes how I feel
Blue is my favourite colour.

Brad Culbertson (10)
Macosquin Primary School, Coleraine

I Am Your Fairy . . .

Glittering, glistening, flying high,
Deeply in love in the dark blue sky,
A sparkle, a twinkle, a wish away are you,
Forever to stay and say;

>   Fly with a twinkle,
>   Fly with me,
>   Fly to the moon,
>   Fly over the sea.

As I awoke at the crack of dawn
The sparkle went and you were born,
You are my sunlight, moon and star,
And I am your fairy locked up in a jar,
My wish is clear for you to say;

>   Fly with a twinkle,
>   Fly with me,
>   Fly to the moon,
>   Fly over the sea
> But most of all set me . . .
>   Free!

Becky Turner (11)
Onchan Primary School, Onchan

Rainbows

Rainbow shining in the sky,
I can't stop staring,
I don't know why.

It's just so colourful,
Everywhere I go,
Even if I'm somewhere I don't know.

I can just imagine it,
The pot of gold,
From the stories I've been told.

Every colour you could think of
It will be there,
Shimmering high up in the air.

When I am looking up to the sky,
At the rainbow standing by,
Oh how I wish I could fly.

Well that's all I have to say
About rainbows of course,
And their colourful way.

Annabel Grainger (11)
Onchan Primary School, Onchan

Henry The Elf

I met an elf in my backyard,
His middle name is Henry,
I really don't know his first name,
He doesn't want to tell me.

He lives in the tall old oak tree,
With a little clockwork mouse,
He often invites me in for tea,
Inside his little house.

Inside it's very pretty,
With sparkles everywhere,
He tells me stories and feeds me cakes,
While I sit in an old armchair.

The armchair I usually sit in,
Is not like any other,
It used to belong to a great old king,
Who inherited it from his brother.

I met an elf in my backyard,
His middle name is Henry,
I really don't know his first name,
He doesn't want to tell me.

Elizabeth Quayle (11)
Onchan Primary School, Onchan

The Bird

As the sun rises
The bird awakens,
Stretching his wings
And starts to fly.

The sun was up
It never went down,
The bird still flying,
Looking around.

Down in the grass
Was a wiggly worm,
The bird went down,
Caught it and turned.

The sun was setting,
The bird flew away
Into his nest
And snuggled away.

Laura Cherry (11)
Onchan Primary School, Onchan

Fairies

'Hello fairies, how do you do?
Feeling a little down or blue?
Are you feeling well my friend?
Let's read a story right to the end!
This one's about the fairy bridge,
The place where you just happen to live.
The main character's name is Princess Rose,
Who lives happy ever after as the story comes to close.
Maybe you could write a story about where you are,
It could be about the people who greet you from their car.
If you do, people will see,
Just how cheerful you can be!'

Sammie Caine (11)
Onchan Primary School, Onchan

Witches

A witch's face is a ghastly sight,
In the deadly dark of night.
Cauldrons, potions, spells, galore,
Which make you cough, sneeze and itch, so sore.

On her broomstick flying high,
In the middle of the dark blue sky.
Flying past the big, bright moon,
Hopefully we'll be back soon.

Their noses are pointy,
Covered in warts,
When they laugh
All you hear is a snort.

Their fingers are curled up
Just like cats' claws,
They should be walking,
On all fours.

They have no toes,
Just flat stumps,
Just looking at them,
Gives you goosebumps.

That's the end of my poem about a witch,
If they harm you, you'll need more than one stitch!

Gemma Granger (11)
Onchan Primary School, Onchan

Spinosaurus

Spinosaurus, Spinosaurus, you're very, very bright,
Maybe if you stand in the dark you'll still glow with light,
Spinosaurus, Spinosaurus, you've got very large jaws,
With very long arms you have very long claws,
Spinosaurus, Spinosaurus, you may be very strong,
But up against Tyrannosaurus you won't last too long.

James Sayle (11)
Onchan Primary School, Onchan

Witches Are . . .

Witches are creepy,
They fly around at night,
They're so ugly,
Your eyes hurt at their sight.

Their noses are pointed,
Their hats are black,
They make potions,
So you wouldn't want to mess with her cat.

They make up riddles
And they dance around fires,
They're so stupid,
Their grammar is dire.

They hide behind hats and capes,
They live on their own,
If you see their fingers,
It looks like they have been sewn.

Jessica Duncan (11)
Onchan Primary School, Onchan

The Evil Cyber Robot

The robot has no arms and legs but it has a head,
At night he keeps sleeping on my bed.
One morning it followed me to the fair,
It stole my hot dog and it didn't share,
It turned larger but I didn't care.
It tried to destroy our town,
The sparks and electricity sparkled all around,
There's nothing left.
Then the world was destroyed and there's nothing here.

Phiranat Khamnok (11)
Onchan Primary School, Onchan

The Wind

The wind is full of magical things,
It's made up from pixies and fairy kings,
It's full of butterflies and special gold,
The wind is flowing and sometimes cold.

Wind can blow anything away,
The wind is a ghost, so they say,
If you look close into the wind,
You'll see the colours and how it spins.

When you say 'I hate the wind',
A pixie's life turns rather grim,
The pixie grows lots of hair,
(But some don't mind and some don't care).

And if you hate the wind,
You'll be hating the world of magical things,
So when you hear the wind rush past,
Don't say you hate it so very fast.

Aalish Foulger (11)
Onchan Primary School, Onchan

The Dragon Castle

As he stepped onto the bridge he heard a creak,
The bridge wobbled side to side which made him shriek.
He crossed it at a slow speed,
At the end he saw some bones and meat,
So he went in and grabbed his sword,
But dropped it on the tiled floor.

He stepped into the room,
And saw an orange gloom,
He saw a dragon flying round and round,
They had a fight but the dragon came down,
He went up to the tower,
Found the ring and came down with power.

Kieran Moore (11)
Onchan Primary School, Onchan

Pixies And Fairies

Pixie dust is in the air,
It makes you sneeze everywhere,
All the pixies in the world,
Gathered together with their wings so curled.

Everyone that comes today,
Chanting happily away, away,
All the sun and moon and rain,
Come together to visit Spain.

Over the bridge and away they go,
Awfully quietly and awfully slow,
Over the bridge and to the magic field,
Giving their presents on the road they kneeled.

At the end of the day,
When all the enemies are away,
Into the sky on their flying cow,
The fairies and pixies have to go now!

Lily Purdy (11)
Onchan Primary School, Onchan

Fairies

I am a fairy spinning around,
My feet will never touch the ground,
So many things I see on my way,
I will never see them in a normal day.

Glittering up in the blue sky,
This feeling I hope will never die,
My wings spread out, the wind in my face,
I fly slowly, it's not a race.

I am flying high and then I stop,
I get put into a jar then suddenly drop,
I have been in this jar for more than a day
I just feel like I should fly away.

Lorna Griffiths (11)
Onchan Primary School, Onchan

The Joy Of Jelly

Jelly, jam tarts,
Cranberries and cream,
Mix them all together,
And it will be a dream.

Toffee, treacle,
Sticky and sweet,
If you blend them all up,
It will be a treat.

Pineapples, purple plums,
Lemons and lime,
If you find them nice,
You will have a great time.

Raspberries, raisins,
Marmalade and mustard,
Get a roly poly pud,
And even add some custard.

Strawberries, sensational,
Add chocolate sauce and chew,
It will be an utter delight,
Especially for you.

Laura Atkinson (11)
Onchan Primary School, Onchan

Gruesome Land

Gruesome goblins,
Gruesome ogres,
Eyeball soup,
Snot and bones,
Smelly socks,
Smelly feet,
Mouldy meat,
Mouldy sheep,
Mouldy people in the deep,
Lonely ears without a head,
Lonely nose without a face,
Blood and guts without a corpse,
Without an ugly man,
Without an ugly woman,
They could never accomplish this,
With the goblins,
With the ogres,
I bid you goodnight,
And one more thing,
It's all the same in gruesome land.

Ryan Jones (11)
Onchan Primary School, Onchan

Sun

The sun up so very high
Started falling down from the sky
It was time to flee
When it hit the sea
What a crazy day, oh my!

Megan McMylor (11)
Padfield Community Primary School, Padfield

The Car Kennings

Wheel spinner
Sharp turner
Fast braker
Ticket maker
Big speeder
Stiff rider
Record braker
Quick accelerator.

Cameron Neve (11)
Padfield Community Primary School, Padfield

Blue

Blue is the colour of my uniform,
Blue is the flowing sea,
Blue is the sky so high,
Blue is the colour of my eyes,
Blue is the one I like,
Blue is the colour of the school walls,
Blue is the colour of my clothes,
Blue is the colour of my friend's schoolbag,
Blue is the colour of the light summer rain,
Blue is the colour of many things!

Shannon Hazlett (10)
Poyntzpass Primary School, Newry

Autumn

A nimals prepare for winter
U nder the trees the leaves fall
T he harvest is gathered in
U p in the hills I bring the cattle in
M any lovely colours, red, yellow and gold
N othing so beautiful as autumn.

Jacob Cairns (10)
Poyntzpass Primary School, Newry

Blue Is . . .

Blue is the colour of the dark sea,
Blue is the colour of the sky,
Blue is the colour of the clouds that go by,
Blue is the colour of the car we have,
Blue is the colour of the walls in the classroom,
Blue is the colour of our school uniform,
Blue is the colour of the books that we write in,
Blue is the colour of my eyes,
Blue is the colour of a Chelsea football top,
Blue is the colour of a tiny bird's egg.

Emma Liggett (11)
Poyntzpass Primary School, Newry

My View Of A Cow

A grass muncher,
A milk producer,
A cud chewer,
A big animal,
A field lover,
A hay grazer,
A beautiful creature,
A friendly thing.

James Thompson (10)
Poyntzpass Primary School, Newry

A Recipe For A Summer's Day

Take a hot sun,
And a clear sky.
Add a cool drink,
Sprinkle with sunlight.
Cover with suncream
And wrap with ice cubes,
To make a summer's day.

Matthew Patterson (11)
Poyntzpass Primary School, Newry

My View Of A Bear

A long snout,
A honey lover,
A loud growler,
A short neck,
A fat stomach,
A short tail,
A warm coat,
A big mouth.

Ashley Morrow (10)
Poyntzpass Primary School, Newry

My View Of A Rabbit

A carrot muncher,
A happy hopper,
A burrow hider,
A fast runner,
A hunted creature,
A fluffy tail,
A cabbage lover,
A cuddly friend.

Matthew Denny (11)
Poyntzpass Primary School, Newry

My View Of A Hippopotamus

An enormous mammal,
A grey creature,
A gigantic head,
A super swimmer,
A heavy mover,
A heat lover,
A food gobbler.

Robbie Clarke (11)
Poyntzpass Primary School, Newry

Laughing Cow

One summer's day in the month of May,
I put my pink glossy wellies on
To go and play amongst the hay
Down in the meadow.

I skipped through the field of wild daisies,
And to my surprise I nearly died
When I saw a cow in her disguise.

The laughing cow with her silly hat
Was singing and dancing
Like a litter of cats.

Her black spots had turned to pink instead,
To match the bonnet on her head,
She laughed as she fell to the ground
As she saw birds flying round and round.

I stood and watched, my mouth open wide,
I couldn't believe what was in front of my eyes,
The laughing cow in her disguise!

Jillian Wilson (10)
Poyntzpass Primary School, Newry

My View Of A Lizard

A tricky creature
A small animal
A camouflaging magician
A selfish eater
A climbing critter
A scaly stalker
An aggressive hunter.

Chelsea Ellison (10)
Poyntzpass Primary School, Newry

Evacuation, Evacuation

Evacuation, evacuation
Everyone is sad.
No one likes it and nor do I.

People shoving,
Talking with sadness,
Some with excitement but no laughter.

Mum and Dad wave
I start to cry,
I tell myself
No crying, no crying.

I get to the train
Guards are at the doors,
They scare me
And then it happens.

Christopher Smart (9)
Poyntzpass Primary School, Newry

Evacuation

I am scared, walking through all these people.
They keep coming up to me,
Looking at my label and saying no.

Now I am on the train
A family has got me.
We are on our way to their house.

We arrive, it's such a big house,
I cannot believe I'm here.

I am inside the house now,
I do not know where to go.
I find my bedroom,
It seems enormous.

Judith Alderdice (10)
Poyntzpass Primary School, Newry

A Recipe For A Summer's Day

Take a pair of sunglasses
And a towel and suncream.
Add a pair of swimming trunks and flip-flops.
Sprinkle with seawater and sand,
Cover with shells and pebbles
And wrap in a bucket and spade
To make a summer's day.

Ryan McClure (10)
Poyntzpass Primary School, Newry

Autumn

A utumn leaves are falling
U p in the sky, swallows fly away
T he farmer ploughs his fields
U sing a John Deere tractor
M ornings are getting colder
N ights are getting darker.

Ross McMullan (10)
Poyntzpass Primary School, Newry

Green Is . . .

Green is the colour of grass,
Green is the colour of the army,
Green is the colour of a colouring pencil,
Green is the colour of mouldy cheese,
Green is the colour of toxic waste,
Green is the colour of my friend's sharpener.

Russell Graham (10)
Poyntzpass Primary School, Newry

Winter

W hen the frost comes
I go to the shop to buy a coat and hat
N ow the dark nights get colder
T rees whistling in the wind
E venings in by a nice warm fire
R ain, sleet and snow arrive.

Richard Corry (10)
Poyntzpass Primary School, Newry

Bats

Black bats
Hairy, scary
They like to bite your legs
They are always flapping their wings
Black bats.

Ben Lawrence (8)
St John's CE Primary School, Burscough

Chocolate

There was a young man called Jake
Who ate a giant chocolate cake.
He went up a hill
Fell and needed a pill
And his friend bought him a flake.

Ryan Byrne (8)
St John's CE Primary School, Burscough

Autumn - Haiku

Brown leaves swirl and twirl
They crunch underneath my feet
Autumn is here now.

Emma Leary (9)
St John's CE Primary School, Burscough

Everton FC - Cinquain

The Blues
Shirts always blue
Except when we're away
When we score - brilliant goals, wow!
Class team!

Joshua Birchall (9)
St John's CE Primary School, Burscough

Tractor - Cinquain

Tractor
Chugging along
Silence, the engine stopped
Oh no, it had run out of oil
Motor.

Ellie Gorton (9)
St John's CE Primary School, Burscough

Chris

There once was a boy called Chris,
He never took a shot and missed,
One day he tried
And then he cried,
'Oh no I missed!'

Jack Winders (9)
St John's CE Primary School, Burscough

Limerick

There was a young man called Jake
One day he saw a grass snake
He ran away to hide
Then there was a landslide
Jake ended up like a pancake.

Andrew Hawick (9)
St John's CE Primary School, Burscough

Jake

There was a young man called Jake
And he wanted to go to the lake
He put on his coat
And got in his boat
And then had a milkshake.

Tara Davies (8)
St John's CE Primary School, Burscough

Football - Cinquain

Football
It's really fun
Have a really great time
I love football, so do a lot
Round ball.

Charlotte Booth (8)
St John's CE Primary School, Burscough

Limerick

There was a young man called Jake
Who went fishing in a lake
He caught a fish
And had it for tea on a dish
Then he'd eat a chocolate flake.

Hayley Medlock (9)
St John's CE Primary School, Burscough

Puppies - Cinquain

Puppies
Some have short hair
Jump, roll, shake everywhere
Cuddly, caring, loving puppies
Canine.

Sarah Baker (9)
St John's CE Primary School, Burscough

Different People

D ifferent people, doesn't matter
I n different countries living happily
V arieties of people
E motions are different as well
R aining in different countries
S ad and happy at different times
I ntelligence doesn't matter, it's the care that God gives us
T iny and big, all different
Y oung and old.

Stephen French (9)
Thongsley Fields Primary & Nursery School, Huntingdon

You Can Be ABC

An amazing airline pilot or a brave boxer,
A clumsy cricketer or a dirty digger,
An evil educator or a furious footballer,
A grumpy gardener or a humorous human,
An ignorant investigator or a joking judge,
A karate king or a lucky lecturer,
A magical magician or a nosey neighbour,
An original optician or a personal producer,
A quality quack doctor or a running riddler,
A silly scientist or a terrific storyteller,
An underground umpire or a van-driving vicar,
A wonderful watcher or an 'xpert X-rayer,
A young yak milker or a zany zoologist.

Lauren Whitham (9)
Thongsley Fields Primary & Nursery School, Huntingdon

Puppy

   Cheeky teaser
Cat chaser
   Fierce hunter
Warm snuggler
   Good jumper.

Aisha Russell (8)
Thongsley Fields Primary & Nursery School, Huntingdon

Today I Feel As . . .

Happy as the sun
Funny as a clown
Baked as a bun
Creased as a frown
Sharp as a sword.

Jack James (9)
Thongsley Fields Primary & Nursery School, Huntingdon

Mouse

Noisy squeaker
Hole liver
Cheese eater
Cat hider
Quick runner
People scarer.

Carwyn Kelly (9)
Thongsley Fields Primary & Nursery School, Huntingdon

Today I Feel As . . .

Happy as a movie star
Wavy as the sea
As sharp as a stag
As small as a pea
Clever as a butterfly
As brave as a knight
As silly as a baby
Cute as a fairy.

Melissa Seymour (9)
Thongsley Fields Primary & Nursery School, Huntingdon

Fire

Fire is like a hungry monster.
Flames are like a fireball,
And it burns everything in its way.
Fire is like a fiery volcano.
When fire is gone it smells of smoke.
Smoke you can't see through and
Sometimes it can kill you.
And sometimes it can get in your lungs
And kill you.

Shaun Beardsley (9)
West Jesmond Primary School, Newcastle upon Tyne

The World's Disasters

An earthquake is a child in a tantrum
A tsunami cuts his knee, he cries and the waves fly up.

Disasters can happen!

A tornado is a child having an asthma attack,
A gale is a child breathing out.

Disasters can happen!

A volcano erupting is a child with a rumbling stomach,
A mudslide is a messy eater,
An avalanche is a child bellowing.

Disasters can happen!

A thunderstorm is a child grumbling,
A blizzard is a child sneezing.

Disasters can happen!

William Haigh (9)
West Jesmond Primary School, Newcastle upon Tyne

Air

Air is a bubbly breathing breeze
That we breathe in and out.
Air makes you very very fresh.
It is really important to everyone.
Without it everyone will be dead.
That's why everyone is alive.
And living their life happily.

It can be strong sometimes
So it can blow everything.
Sometimes it can be calm,
Sometimes it can be soft and gentle.

Aya Hegab (10)
West Jesmond Primary School, Newcastle upon Tyne

Air

As the year begins
The air is cold,
A frozen gale,
The icy breeze stings like an invisible bee,
The wind,
An angry storm,
Ripping through the freezing air,
Devouring the Earth
Yet as the seasons turn
The wind evolves into a gentle breeze,
Brushing softly through its vast emptiness
And as the leaves begin to fall
The sky turns
Crimson-red.
With the sun a glowing ember
Illuminating the air's great planet.

Jonah Vinsome (10)
West Jesmond Primary School, Newcastle upon Tyne

The Speech Of A . . .

You can't touch me, but I can touch you.
I am swirling and twirling, twisting and turning
Towards your homes,
And when I touch you, I blast you up my enormous pipe
Making you feel small.
I take a secret path that no one has or will discover.
Come with no warning.
I am deadly and strong.
I am also angry at you humans that took control of my property.
Therefore I attack.
So get out of my path,
If you want to live,
Because I am the most violent force on Earth . . .
I am a tornado.

Horia Dragoi (9)
West Jesmond Primary School, Newcastle upon Tyne

The Wind Is Getting Stronger

Acrobatic air
Lifts leaves.

Winding winds
Hug hats.

Gurgling gales
Push people.

Troublesome tornadoes
Terrorise towns.

Horrendous hurricanes
Crush cities.

Extra electricity is
Created by wind.

Extra winds are created
By electricity.

So everybody gets something
In the end.

Charles Antons (10)
West Jesmond Primary School, Newcastle upon Tyne

Earth

I feel busy people with their tickling feet,
And crawling animals that people beat.
I cannot see because I've got no eyes
But I do have friends to your surprise.
My friends are Mars and also Venus,
But they're too far to come and see us.
From the outside, I look like a big blue and white ball,
But really I think I'm very small.
I am a tremendous playground where you can play
And I'm full of life, every night and day.

Lydia Reeve (9)
West Jesmond Primary School, Newcastle upon Tyne

Earth, Earth

Earth, Earth, nice Earth
Rocks falling down the cliff
Mountain tops exploding
Sand washing up on the beach.

Earth, Earth, beautiful Earth
Coal being mined
Animals gobbling plants
Woods growing big.

Earth, Earth, brave Earth
Life growing on the planet
Bugs buzzing around
Elephants flapping their ears.

Earth, Earth, strong Earth
People walking around
Children playing games
Living happily on the ground.

Earth, Earth, violent Earth
Earthquakes cracking away
Volcanoes blasting
Life dying.

Ruairidh Chester (9)
West Jesmond Primary School, Newcastle upon Tyne

Fire, Fire, Fire . . .

Fire is a flickering flame
But not a game.
A candle is lit
And then you could sit.

The darkness has come
And there is . . . oh my, oh my, a terrible flame
Then the darkness ends.

Zulekha Sadiq (10)
West Jesmond Primary School, Newcastle upon Tyne

The Candle

Fire is a quiet, calm flame flittering in the dark house
The flame on the candle feels lonely and upset
It sees a mouse crawling freely
It wants to be free as well
It shakes itself to fall to the ground
And lands with a silent pound
And out of that small flame comes dancing fire all around.

It burns and kills all furniture around
And makes everything fall to the ground
Now the hot wild fire turns the solids into ashes
The fire wants to do some bashing
So bashes and burns all tables and chairs
And spreads itself everywhere.

The fire heard a *nee-nar* noise
But carries on burning the house
Oh no, the fire engine's coming
What do we do?
The fireman blasts his hosepipe
And now the fire will die.

Aisha Omer-Hellings (10)
West Jesmond Primary School, Newcastle upon Tyne

The Life Of Water

I am like a giant bath
Surrounding your islands,
You often swim in me, splash in me, jump in me.
I drip on you, wet you,
I sometimes drown you but I regret when I do.
I splash against the solid rocks,
I'm cold and speedy when I rush up as waves.
I am a blue, blurry blob floating around.
You pollute me but you make me rise.
I am a wonder of the world.

Robert Kreibich (9)
West Jesmond Primary School, Newcastle upon Tyne

House On Fire

No one knows how it started,
The house caught fire,
Demolishing everything in its path,
Rising higher and higher.

The house surrendering,
Burning to remains,
Feeling all alone,
Suffering all the pains.

Fire never giving up
Until the house is gone,
Eliminating happy memories,
Feeling really strong.

Letting nothing pass without suffering,
Fire running wild,
He's happy until,
999 is dialled.

Sirens coming,
Fire engines here,
Look closely at the fire,
It's trembling with fear.

Wiping away the anger,
Being really brave,
Sending the fire off,
To its smoky grave!

Molly O'Brien (10)
West Jesmond Primary School, Newcastle upon Tyne

A Tidal Wave

I come unexpected
Crashing and splashing
Onto the beach,
I am life-threatening
Torturing,
Terrorising
And scary.
I make people run
And scream.
Children feel small
Like tiny insects
Because I am the
King of kings.
I am a flood of unwanted deaths
For I am a
Tidal wave!

Emily Armitage (10)
West Jesmond Primary School, Newcastle upon Tyne

The Burning Sun

Fire is the burning sun
It makes sweat run, run, run.
It's a dangerous demon
Miles from the sky
Destroys all in its way
I don't know why
A glowing light
When it's alight
It stings when it's touched
More than a bit.

Day after day it kills anyway
You can't stop it
    It's fire!

Rayyan Qureshi (10)
West Jesmond Primary School, Newcastle upon Tyne

The Fire Goblin

As the city slept,
The fire goblin came,
Decided to start his wicked plot,
And get London screaming, screaming, screaming
And get London screaming.

So he crept off to the baker's shop,
To where it all began,
He touched the wax, he touched the wood,
And anything that burns, burns, burns.

After an hour he heard a shriek
Which made him laugh and dance
It also made him leap and cackle
Jump with joy, joy, joy.
Jump with joy.

Someone yelled,
Someone screamed,
Someone shouted,
'The fire goblin's back.'

Sophie Neibig (10)
West Jesmond Primary School, Newcastle upon Tyne

Pollution In The Air

In the city factory chimneys churn out smoke
All the smog makes you cough and choke
Petrol fumes, car exhausts
Leaving a gap in the ozone layer of course.
Too many people, too much pollution
I wonder - *what is the solution?*

In the country wide open spaces
Everyone knows all the faces
White fluffy clouds, beautiful blue sky
Makes you wish you could fly
The breeze is fresh and the air is clean.

Ella Davenport (9)
West Jesmond Primary School, Newcastle upon Tyne

Fire, Fire, Fire!

I am a blazing velocity,
A ruthless murderer, a dangerous predator,
A tedious conflagration,
A am a seething wall of blistering flame,
I am a bloodthirsty king, terrorising my world,
Fear creeps round every corner, should I be there,
You cannot hold me in your creamy pale hands,
For that they would become crinkly and scorched.
Hatred is my only strength,
Water is my only weakness,
For when it comes at me, gushing like a screaming horror,
I shrivel up, die, wither for the rest of eternity,
I belong to the world,
Yet I belong to no one,
I am a treacherous destroyer,
A lonely traveller, a forgotten god,
My hatred is the only thing keeping me alive,
Without it, I would be merely a spark, a dying ember.

Valeria Laird (10)
West Jesmond Primary School, Newcastle upon Tyne

Fire Is Hot

Fire is a flame ready to spark
Fire is a devil laughing
Fire is a burning sausage
Fire smells like a smoking kettle.

Fire is a heat machine
Fire will burn you and hurt you
Fire is a glittering, glistening, great sparkler
Trying to impress you.

Fire will harm you, hurt you and thrill you.

Fire is hot
You better not . . .

Gaby Knops (10)
West Jesmond Primary School, Newcastle upon Tyne

Lost!

I'm lost in the raving, roaring, blue crinkling paper.
I'm lost on the sea.
I feel your strength through my fingertips,
You carry cancer, malaria and heart disease on your back.
You could violently crush my small and insignificant village
With your fingernail, it would be too easy for you.
                  Crash
                      Bang
                          Wallop
                          You smack me,
With your slippery, slimy, sloppy, icy hands.
But oh beautiful all the creatures of the ocean are here,
              No one is here, yet I might as well
                        Whack!
                            I'm lost inside the raving,
                            Roaring, blue, crinkling paper
                            I'm lost in the sea . . .

Rachel Jacques (9)
West Jesmond Primary School, Newcastle upon Tyne

Air Is What I Am!

I am a friend of the world,
You cannot see me,
But I'm always here,
Right beside you but you cannot flee,
Please don't fear!

If I turn into a deadly twister,
Victory is my goal.
I change into a global devil,
On my war zone stroll!
But careful boys and careful girls this is my first level,
Locked inside your basement now?
Here I come, here I come, here I come!

Lucy Dinsdale (9)
West Jesmond Primary School, Newcastle upon Tyne

Incredible Fire

The fire changes shape all the time,
It could be useful,
It might be horrible,
Usually it spreads all over the place.
It creeps through
The forest as bright
As the sun, dangerous,
Disgusting, demolishing
Water kills the fire.

It whooshes everywhere,
Destroying the fire, killing it dead.

It can attack you.

It could
Follow you everywhere,
It lurks in the darkness,
Careful where you go,
Never touch the yellow flame
Of the fire dying into the last timbers
Of its life, it dies then
And other fires shall emerge.
It could die in Hell.

I am fire!

David Goodwin (9)
West Jesmond Primary School, Newcastle upon Tyne

Natural Elements

Fire is a passionate roaring red making illusions in your mind.
It is a hawk of death and destruction.
Water is a murdering lion clawing a buffalo.
It is a glistening gem, priceless and rare.
Earth is a wild pony bucking away its worries.
It is like a spherical light illuminating everything, magnificently.
Air is a cat purring softly at its owner.

Max Parker (10)
West Jesmond Primary School, Newcastle upon Tyne

Tornadoes Are Like . . .

Tornadoes are like a big raging bull,
Making the skies turn grey and dull.

Tremendous tornadoes terrify trembling townspeople.

Tornadoes are like a massive monster
Eliminating anything in its path.

Tornadoes are like large nuclear bombs
Annihilating Planet Earth.

Tornadoes' favourite place is near the south coast,
This is where they attack and destroy the most.

Tremendous tornadoes terrify trembling townspeople.

Tornadoes are like huge, swirling sandstorms
Demolishing, demolishing houses and farms.

Tornadoes are like giant cobras
Curling around their prey.

Tornadoes are like large cannonballs of air
Smashing into their target.

Tremendous tornadoes terrify trembling townspeople.

William Green (9)
West Jesmond Primary School, Newcastle upon Tyne

Water

The boat floating in the water
Drizzle, drizzle, the rain is falling
The fish flowing in the water
The animals rushing like they're having a race
Kerplush, the dolphins are jumping
Swoosh, swoosh, the waves come, *crash,* they hit the rocks.
I threw a stone in the water then the water goes *plop.*
Splash! I do a bomb in the water.
Ripple, ripple, the water is vibrating.
As the rain is falling, it looks like the water is flooding.

Berina Stitkovac (10)
West Jesmond Primary School, Newcastle upon Tyne

The Flame

The naked candle owns a flame that shimmers in the dark.
It is both elegant and graceful
As it flickers against the shadow cast.

Held in slavery, burning away, the flame decides to strike back.
A spark falls from the mantelpiece, just missing the cat.

It lands directly on the rug, dancing silently with joy,
Then, *crackle, hiss,* it multiplies,
A whole army has formed.

The group of flames grows higher, spreading far and wide,
Then sudden disappointment as the flames start to die.

With a *splish, splash* of water, the flames are nearly out,
Until all that remains is a tiny spark of life,
Glowing dim as an ember.

Raz Gharbi (10)
West Jesmond Primary School, Newcastle upon Tyne

What Is Known Of The Sea

The whoosh as sharks go thundering by
As they destroy the water in front of them.

The octopus swirls around as cool as a cucumber
To produce black foam which stays there for minutes on end.

The fish flutter by with no worry in the world
But the sharks which lurk beyond the gloomy water.

The furious waves get built up by the heavy downfall of rain
Until it crashes down into the swirling water below.

A big, dangerous whirlpool fizzing with icy broth
Surrounded by immense waves
Collects its victims by the dozen.

Big, blue and boisterous swirling water goes round and round
The jagged rocks waiting for someone else's fate.

Adam O'Mara (10)
West Jesmond Primary School, Newcastle upon Tyne

Sparkling, Wavy Water

Glittering, turquoise, lively, whooshes by
With a long-living heart it never cries,
In a world of itself it splashes around,
Its cold explosion slaps my face.
Gracefully as it calms down,
Puffing swirls, swivel around,
Its lullaby song rocks me to sleep,
A peaceful song that I can keep.
The insignificant fish feel lonely and betrayed,
Because everyone's admiring the water they live in.
Water is like a blue frothy ice cream
Waiting to be swooshed up by the clouds.
Way up high.
And as the day turns into night the water
Once more lonely lies . . .
Glittering turquoise, lively, whooshes by
With a long-living heart it never
Cries!

Rachel Laidler (10)
West Jesmond Primary School, Newcastle upon Tyne

Hurricane, Hurricane

Hurricane, hurricane
Has the force of a rocket taking off

Hurricane, hurricane
Is the ultimate storm and always wins the battle!

Hurricane, hurricane
Is getting lonely so he calls his friend, Thunder
To help him attack!

Meanwhile
Meanwhile
The hurricane's full, he says
Goodbye to his friend, Thunder
And waits for another day!

Henry Winter (9)
West Jesmond Primary School, Newcastle upon Tyne

What Does Water Do?

Water, water, why do you kill?
Threaten the lives of humans,
And strangle them and whisk them away,
Until they're finally out of breath and die.

Water, water, you also bring life,
To many creatures that live in the sea.
Such as dolphins, starfish and sea horses,
They all live in the cold, cold sea.

Water, water, don't make tsunamis!
It will make millions of people die,
Children will lose their parents,
And ruin the world's precious land.

Water, water, you help us to live,
Give us plenty of fresh water,
To cook, to drink, to wash ourselves,
And have fun in the swimming pool.

      Water, water, thanks for all!

Emma Sin Yee Lip (10)
West Jesmond Primary School, Newcastle upon Tyne

Air

Air is cold and hot and sometimes normal.
We breathe out air and we breathe in air.
Air is fresh and air is dusty.
Air is just on Earth, not on other planets.
Strong air makes people fly away,
Strong air causes lots of damage.
Strong air makes houses fly away,
Strong air makes trees fly away,
Strong air makes windows fly away.
Strong air makes bricks fall off the wall.
Now air is calm and soft and white,
Everyone has a normal life again.

Saman Karimi (9)
West Jesmond Primary School, Newcastle upon Tyne

Fire Is . . .

Fire is yellow, orange, red and blue
Fire is as red as blood
Fire is a burning sun
Fire is like a dragon's breath
Fire is the Devil
Fire's weakness is water
Fire is the burning houses
Fire is death
Fire is Hell
Fire is yellow, orange, red and blue
Fire, fire, fire.

Fire is burning flames
Fire is water's strength
Fire is the touch of death
Fire is a warning bell
Fire is a dreadful yell
Fire is burning flames
Fire, fire, fire.

Matthew Moore (10)
West Jesmond Primary School, Newcastle upon Tyne

Water

You cannot walk on me
You just sink
You drink me sometimes
If I'm clean and clear.

Drown you if I can
Icy cold, I freeze you
A rushing, rippling, raging river
Crashing and cascading
Down, down, down.

Until my journey comes to an end
I am water.

Gerry Rowland (9)
West Jesmond Primary School, Newcastle upon Tyne

Underground Experience

I am trapped,
I hear the drip, drip
Of condensation from the rocks,
I feel hot, humid, hostile,
It's unbearable down here,
I see nothing but darkness
And the outline of crumbling rocks,
I taste the air around me
As disgusting as
Molten sick,
I smell something,
Something,
Something,
I know what
I smell
Earth.

Sophie Barker (10)
West Jesmond Primary School, Newcastle upon Tyne

My Journey

Drip, drop, plip, plop,
I come down.

Pitter-patter, splitter, splatter,
I start my journey down.

Into the sea I travel,
I'm a giant roaring wave,
I'm a destructive, destroying tidal wave,
I'm a tsunami galloping through the sky,
As I fiercely pass by.

Or am I?

I'm refreshing, I'm gentle,
I'm a matter between life and death,
I'm water.

Elliott Dixon (9)
West Jesmond Primary School, Newcastle upon Tyne

A Picture

The Earth is like a watercolour painting,
The colours blending into each other,
While the brush jerks across the paper,
Splodge, splodge, splodge.

The Earth is a volcano erupting,
Spilling blue, green and brown lava into one corner of space,
Plip, plop, splish, splosh.

The Earth is like a huge, beady eagle eye,
Constantly rolling its big blue, green and brown eyeball
To his neighbours.

For some, Earth is a happy place,
A joyful place to live,
But for others, Earth is a sad, greedy place that no one deserves,
Tut, tut, tut.

For one part of the planet the places are full of poverty,
But the other part of the planet is popular with people,
Who aren't always polite and patient,
And plants, water and food shouldn't be taken for granted.

The Earth has warmth from fire,
The Earth has food from air,
The Earth has its freshness from water,
But fire, water and air don't have each other without Earth.

Yasmina Carlton (10)
West Jesmond Primary School, Newcastle upon Tyne

Fire

A candle flame flickering, fighting against water.
A gun firing, flaming, fading, gone.
Furnace flames fleeing from water.
Furry animals flee from forest fires.
Fierce flames flitter from fireplace to fireplace.
Ferocious fires frolic freeing flames
Frightened flames flee from water.

Jamie Meikle (10)
West Jesmond Primary School, Newcastle upon Tyne

I'm A Drip Of Water

I'm a drip of water,
I fall from the sky,
I'm getting to the ground now,
Bye, bye, bye!

I'm getting to a lake now,
I'm flowing to the sea,
I can see a tidal wave,
Oh no, it's going for me!

It's getting really close now,
I'm getting very scared,
I need my mummy here,
Because she's the one that cares.

Whoosh, crash, aahh that was fun!
I don't know why I was scared,
Water's like a sweet-smelling bun,
I took my chance, I'm so glad I dared!

Hattie Airey (10)
West Jesmond Primary School, Newcastle upon Tyne

The Flame!

Fire from a volcano
Flickers around
Turns into ashes
And then hits the ground.

When it hits the ground,
The flicker vanishes,
The beautiful flame extinguishes.

Now the flame has extinguished
And we are safe,
We can stop running to
A protective place.

Aaliyah Khan (10)
West Jesmond Primary School, Newcastle upon Tyne

The Rolling Blue

Water rushes through the trees,
Going forward with the breeze,
Swoosh, woosh, swish.

Rolling waves across the sea,
Racing ripples all so free,
Flicker, sprinkle, sparkle.

Seaweed up and on the shore,
Like a wig upon the floor,
Crisp, crackle, crack.

Rain is falling on the ground,
Puddles forming all around,
Drizzle, drip, plip.

Whirlpools dance about inside,
The crystal water flies and glides,
Twist, toss, turn.

Water travels everywhere,
On the ground and in the air!

Chloe Wilson (10)
West Jesmond Primary School, Newcastle upon Tyne

Earth

Earth is like a big balloon bouncing around in space.
Earth is a blue, shimmering sea and green grassy fields.
Earth is terrible traffic trapped at the traffic lights.
Chatting people, laughing people, waiting patiently for
                                                        their time to go.
Earth is like a football, big and round.
Earth is shivering cool, but boiling hot as well.
Earth would not be the same without us.

Zoe Hovells (10)
West Jesmond Primary School, Newcastle upon Tyne

Fire

Fire is like a deadly disease
That can never be cured.

Fire reminds people of anger
And aggression.

Fire looks like the sun galloping
Through the sky at the speed of light.

Fire is fireworks spluttering in the sky
As a blistering spark of light.

Fire does the Devil's dirty work
In an instant.

Fire takes people's lives slowly and painfully.

Fire has a sense of belonging
And warmth.

But most important of all,
Fire is a killer.

Tamandeep Singh Lally (9)
West Jesmond Primary School, Newcastle upon Tyne

Water Cycle

Drip, drop, I fall to the ground,
Trickle, splick, I wriggle my way down.
Splish, splosh, I swim into a river,
Blishsh, bsh, I've got friends that are much bigger!
Fwoosh, flop, down the mountainside,
Shwish, shwish, I go roly-poly bye!
Splash, crash, I cascade into a lake,
Swirl, whirl, now I'm wide awake.
Gloosh, bubosh, straight into the sea.
Fizz, pizz, it's all over again for me.

Jessica Peach (9)
West Jesmond Primary School, Newcastle upon Tyne

Earth

If you plant some seeds in me
The grass will grow much greener!

The pollution from cars will cause disaster
To the rainforest
And kill all the trees.
Instead create a garden and grow some crops.

The cars go *crash, bang* and *clang*
In a car crash.
People run and scream and shout,
People walk and slam about,
As cars crash and people go to hospital.

People scream when I cause
A volcano to spurt some lava,
But that is when for some people
It will end.

Becky Franks (9)
West Jesmond Primary School, Newcastle upon Tyne

Fierce Fire

The fire it burns,
So brilliant and bright.
It carries on sparkling,
All through the night.

The colours are red,
Orange and blue,
Ouch! It's hot,
Don't let it burn you.

Fire spreads like water in a bath,
Destroying everything in her path.

Ahmed Bouchelouche (10)
West Jesmond Primary School, Newcastle upon Tyne

H²0, Drip, Drop

The sun melts me,
But I don't care,
I am going to transform from one thing to another,
As I trickle down,
I become a pond.

Drip, drop,
I flow down the mountain,
Splish, splash,
My friends come as well,
Drizzle, drazzle,
I become a lake.

I am rushing now,
Swoosh,
The sound of *pitter-patter* is from miles away
The pressure is on.

Hiisss,
My friends are getting murky,
As well as that,
I've become a river.

I travel along the river,
There is a huge amount of space,
As I am approaching the space,
I get hit by objects,
But I'm no river anymore,
I am the sea.

Some of my friends are gone,
And it'll be all over for me now,
Oh well, I can't wait till next time,
When I'll join them again.

Waleed Saqib (9)
West Jesmond Primary School, Newcastle upon Tyne

The Silent Killer

Fire is a silent assassin creeping up behind people's backs.
Fire spreads like a disease showing no mercy.
It sounds like a crackling cracker cracking.
Smoke is a cigarette, apart from 100 times worse.
Smoke twists and turns, reaching up to the sky like a coiling snake.
Red shows warmth and danger reaching up to you.
Fire warms your Aga up which warms your food.
Fire is a radiator keeping us warm.
Fire is life itself.

Joe Blair (10)
West Jesmond Primary School, Newcastle upon Tyne

The Candle

The candle on the mantelpiece never goes out,
Even if you blow it with all your might.

The wind blows across the empty window sill
And the leaves fall off the trees.

But the candle on the mantelpiece never goes out,
Even if you blow with all your might.

The waves rise and fall, the fish swim and die,
But the candle on the mantelpiece does not go out!

Lucy Chappel (9)
West Jesmond Primary School, Newcastle upon Tyne

Air

Air is cold and hot sometimes.
People are happy when it's hot.
Air is calm and gentle.
Air smells nice sometimes.
If we didn't have air we wouldn't be alive today.
Everybody needs air to breathe.

Haris Ghani (10)
West Jesmond Primary School, Newcastle upon Tyne

Deadly But Gentle

Fire can blaze and flow,
Deadly and dangerous.

Frightening fire, fuming, flaring,
Flickering and flashing.

Wars and guns, inferno and loud,
As fire burns it is tall and proud.

Scarlet, orange, yellow and red,
You can't hide from it in bed!

Shouting, yelling, all the people cheer,
Banging, crashing as fireworks appear.

Warm, flickering in the fire,
Quietly, sizzling, something to admire . . .

Liberty Smart (9)
West Jesmond Primary School, Newcastle upon Tyne

Water

Splish-splash, goes the rain on a wet day,
Sun goes in, umbrellas go out,
Children jump in puddles with wellies on,
Rain tapping on a window sounds like
Someone knocking on a door.

Sometimes the sea can be very scary,
Like the tsunami, the sea gets sucked up,
Like someone drinking a glass of water,
But then it gets thrown back out and lots of people can die.

Water comes from all sorts of places
Like the sea, taps, sewers and swimming pools.

Water is everywhere!
Water is life!

Chloe McClements (9)
West Jesmond Primary School, Newcastle upon Tyne

Fire

The fire burns,
The fire is a stain.
The fire turns.
It puts you in pain.

Fire cracks, it
Makes impacts.
Fire is quiet,
Fire burns sticks.

The fire colours mix
With red, blue, black,
Yellow, the fire is hot,
Yet still mellow.

Liam Green (10)
West Jesmond Primary School, Newcastle upon Tyne

Water

Drip-drop!
Plip-plop!
I fall to the Earth's surface
There I lie on the mountain tops
Standing as still as I can.
When suddenly *swishhh!*
I'm cascading down the mountain,
I'm a wave!
I'm a tidal wave!
I'm a tsunami!
I can be everything dangerous,
I can also be peaceful.
I'm a lifesaver.

Simon Grabham (10)
West Jesmond Primary School, Newcastle upon Tyne

Fire - The Changer

Fire brings light to the darkness,
Fire brings warmth to the cold,
Fire cooks our food,
Fire bakes our bread,
Fire gives us the life force.

Fire is like a silent assassin,
Fire is like a striking cobra,
Fire is a raging evil,
Fire says, 'I do not forgive,
I do not forget.'

Sam Thompson (10)
West Jesmond Primary School, Newcastle upon Tyne

Sadness

Sad faces on a bad day
The losing team is miserable
Sadness smells like a beautiful flower
It feels very rough
The taste is very nasty.

Ali Osman (7)
West Twyford Primary School, Park Royal

Yellow

The colour of the bright sun in the sky
Yellow is singing sweetly in my mind's ear
And it sings high
The colour yellow is like a lemon tart
Yellow feels like the soft skin of a giraffe
It reminds me of a soft sunflower.

Monica Edwards (7)
West Twyford Primary School, Park Royal

Multicolour

Multicolour is a beautiful colour,
It is wonderful and stripy.
It sounds quiet and calm.
This colour smells sweet and like rose.
The multicolour feels soft, squishy and fluffy
And tastes like chocolate and ice cream.
It reminds me of my birthday.

Zahrah Islam (7)
West Twyford Primary School, Park Royal

Pink

Pink happiness looks like a smiley face,
And sounds like a jolly clown.
It smells like candyfloss,
While feeling like a smooth petal.
Pink happiness tastes like a snowy day but warm
Pink happiness is a relaxing beach.

Shanika Smith (8)
West Twyford Primary School, Park Royal

Black

It looks burnt and cloudy.
Sounding like loud rock and roll.
Smells of hot smoke, swirling thickly,
Feels like a rough ripped piece of paper.
Tastes like spicy food.
It reminds me of the colour of endless space.

Diadean Wazait (8)
West Twyford Primary School, Park Royal

White

White reminds me of freshly fallen snow.
A quiet, peaceful sound.
What a wonderful smell of crisp, clean washing,
The feeling of walking through soft, warm cotton wool,
And the taste of summer, cool ice cream.
A calm feeling inside me.
White.

Kyle Peters-Liverpool (8)
West Twyford Primary School, Park Royal

Pink

It is like a pink dress and fluffy.
It sounds like a trumpet and a king walking down the road.
It smells like a beautiful flower with soft petals.
Yet feels like a rough, ungrateful tree.
Pink tastes like a piece of strawberry shortcake,
Melting in my mouth.
It reminds me of my mum and dad.

Toni Ribezzo (8)
West Twyford Primary School, Park Royal

Light Blue

Light blue looks like a bright sky.
It sounds like bluebells ringing softly.
Blue is a great smell of fresh air.
The taste is blueberries, yummy!
Blue reminds me of stars, shining in the sky.

Zainab Lawi (8)
West Twyford Primary School, Park Royal

Recipe For A Cat Sandwich

A cat sandwich is easy to make,
All you do is simply take
One slice of bread,
One slice of strings,
Some whiskers,
One tail,
One cat,
One piece of ear,
A dash of salt -
That ought to do it
And now comes the problem . . .
Too much stuff in it!

Erion Xhixha (9)
West Twyford Primary School, Park Royal

Pink

Pink makes me excited and happy.
It sounds like a quiet jiggle.
Pink smells sticky and strong
And feels sad and joy.
Pink tastes excellent and delicious.

Anushka Sabapara (8)
West Twyford Primary School, Park Royal

My Mum

You are the blue sky swifting past the ocean sea.
You sing like the souls of Destiny's Child playing on my CD player.
You are the sweet-smelling rice and chicken on my plate.
You are the sizzling Fanta in my glass.
You are the silk covering me from head to toe.
You are the stifling sun in Jamaica warming me.
You are the person that makes me feel excited.

Crystal Toppin (9)
West Twyford Primary School, Park Royal

Cats And Butterflies

Cats
Cuddly and fluffy
Running quickly
As beautiful as summer
I wish I had a cat.

Butterfly
Beautiful and quiet
Flying high
As beautiful as spring
I wish I can catch one.

Adham Chakhachiro (9)
West Twyford Primary School, Park Royal

Sunshine

The sun is hot,
It makes me play basketball.
We will respect you like God,
You feel cuddly,
You are as hot as fire,
The sun makes me relax and cools me down,
It makes me think of Jesus,
If I was the sun I would be happy like God.

Toby Yong (9)
West Twyford Primary School, Park Royal

Fairness

I can see a big sun shining down at me.
A bird tweeting in a tree.
It smells like a Christmas morning.
It feels like a silky curtain.
It tastes like smoked salmon.
I wish everyone could be fair.

Kai Butcher (8)
West Twyford Primary School, Park Royal

Sunshine

Sunshine as hot as chilli sauce
Or fire.
I get so hot
Like a new cake from the oven.
Shall I go surfing at the beach?
Perhaps a water fight
With my friends,
Or making water balloons!
I will definitely need ice cream
And a cool swim.
Finally back home
And to sleep.
Ouch! My sunburn hurts.

Rayeen Rahman (9)
West Twyford Primary School, Park Royal

Untitled

The sun is shining
Shining down on the big Earth
The sun is quite big.

Big is the moon too
Big is like the large black space
Big is like the Earth.

Earth has lots of land
Earth has a lot of countries
Earth has lots of plants.

Plants have lots of kinds
Plants are very beautiful
Plants can be small too.

Haoyang Xu (9)
West Twyford Primary School, Park Royal

Animals

Small kittens
Cuddly and splendid
Running fast
As like a little bunny
If only I could have another.

Big cheetah
Fast and fierce
Leaping along
As like a lion
If only you could keep it as a pet.

Big tiger
Orange and black
Strikes deadly
As like a cat
If only I could stroke them.

Bird
Colourful and sweet
Tweets and flies
Like a cat
If only I could catch one.

Owais Khan (9)
West Twyford Primary School, Park Royal

Happiness

Happiness is when the sun shines on my hair.
I am happy when everyone is happy with me.
I am happy when I see the clouds go by.
Happiness is when I smell the flowers,
And when I feel the smooth grass.
I am happy when I see the trees wave in the wind.
If happiness was a colour it would be yellow.

Matthew Butcher (9)
West Twyford Primary School, Park Royal

Sunshine In The Desert

Hot and hazy
Fried and lazy
I look for water
But there is none.
Suddenly I see it
I run
But it's gone
Vanished . . .
A mirage
Disappeared below the sand.
A skeleton,
White, dry and old,
As white as a bit of paper
Will that be me?

Daniel Mooney (8)
West Twyford Primary School, Park Royal

Happiness

I can see a beautiful swan in a lake
Happiness is ducks quacking on the pond
And a pretty red rose
It feels like a soft feather
And tastes like an ice cream.

Rika Ramesh (8)
West Twyford Primary School, Park Royal

Mini Coopers

Mini Coopers
Shiny and wonderful
Driving fast and furious
You're as colourful as a patchwork quilt
If only I could have one of my own one day!

Alexia Ryan (9)
West Twyford Primary School, Park Royal

School

School is cool,
School is great,
School is where you see your mate.

You can learn there,
You can play there
But you really don't want to stay there.

School is where you eat your lunch,
School is what you want to punch,
School is where you get in trouble,
That is when it bursts your bubble.

Do you like it?
Do you hate it
Or do you just want to break it?

Sometimes it's good,
Sometimes it's bad
But I have to say
It gets really mad!

Lucy O'Driscoll (10)
West Twyford Primary School, Park Royal

Excitement

I can see a big,
Multicoloured spaceship.
Excitement is a great eagle,
Soaring at 100mph.
It smells like the salty sea,
Forming into tigers,
It feels like ice blocks,
Melting slowly,
I can taste sugar,
That has just been made,
I want it forever.

Sebri Addous (9)
West Twyford Primary School, Park Royal

A Bleak Christmas

The snow is falling thick and fast,
Forming a white blanket on the frosty ground.
A snowman standing still and lonely in the yard.

But inside all is merry,
Children are laughing, the fire is burning bright,
The turkey's on the table steaming and enticing.

A robin on the gate outside,
His little redbreast shining
And a sleigh pulled by reindeer
Vanishing into the distance.

Julia Parissien (10)
West Twyford Primary School, Park Royal

A Sunny Day

The sun is shining,
The grass is glowing,
What is missing?

The clouds are upset,
Because it's not their turn to shine.

Everyone's backs will burn,
That's funny.

Oh, what a sunny day!

Siobhan Abrams-Brand (10)
West Twyford Primary School, Park Royal

Happiness

I can see two boys playing with a ball.
I can hear two gunshots, bullets travelling at 4000mph.
Smelling the fresh air, so fresh that it can't be real.
I can feel the wind passing through me very fast.
I can taste a lovely Shawarma, the sauce dripping down my chin.

Kais Al-Kaisi (9)
West Twyford Primary School, Park Royal

What Are Mermaids?

What are mermaids?
They have long straight hair
They look so beautiful with their tail.

What are mermaids?
They have a beautiful tail that shimmers with glitter
They have lovely manners and lovely jewellery to wear.

What are mermaids?
They live underwater in a shimmering underwater palace
Have great clothes to wear and great sequins to put
                                             on the shiny hair.

What are mermaids?
You know now!

Rebecca Cheung (9)
West Twyford Primary School, Park Royal

Orange

Orange looks like the sun on a bright day
The sound of a burning fire
Yet smells of fresh flowers in a meadow
It feels like a sponge, all soggy and wet
Like a chocolate chip cookie with orange slices
Orange reminds me of a picnic.

Michaela Devaughan (8)
West Twyford Primary School, Park Royal

Blue

Blue looks like the deep sea
And sounds like a lion roaring
It smells like a flower
I think it feels like a rough pig
It might taste like a frog's leg.

Jade Cassin (8)
West Twyford Primary School, Park Royal

What's The Fuss About?

What's all the fuss about?
The World Cup today
32 countries
Just coming out to play!

Big cars and superstars
Photograph heaven
Salaries from Hollywood
For Sven's best eleven.

Football or soccer
By any other name
Togo Bonito was . . .
The beautiful game.

Brings back the legends
With working class skill
What else could challenge
The masters of Brazil?

The money and the media
It isn't quite the same
Whatever happened
To the people's game?

Yianick Green-Morrison (10)
West Twyford Primary School, Park Royal

Sadness

Sadness is unhappy and poor
I hear him crying and shouting
It smells like dust and dirt
But feels like concrete and cement
The taste is of wine and water.

Ali Joseph (8)
West Twyford Primary School, Park Royal

Purple

Purple is always feeling ready for anything,
Purple is always happy when his favourite football team scores,
He smells so tasty, as good as a chocolate milkshake
And it feels like touching cotton wool,
Purple tastes like salt and vinegar crisps
And reminds me of strawberry ice cream.

Sean Hatoum (8)
West Twyford Primary School, Park Royal

Pink

Pink is a rage of love
It looks like a shining moon,
Pink feels smooth like chocolate in my hands
And sounds like a cry of joy
Pink tastes like a strawberry
It reminds me of my birthday.

Mitchell Gardner (7)
West Twyford Primary School, Park Royal

Red

Red is a bucket full of blood chilling down my cheek.
She sings sweetly in my ear and she sings high.
Her body smells of lemon pie.
The body of red feels like a soft petal.
It tastes of fresh strawberry.
This poem reminds me of a silky, soft flower.

Faith Allen (8)
West Twyford Primary School, Park Royal

Insects

Insects, insects, where could they be?
Insects, insects under the tree.
Beautiful butterflies fluttering by
Wasps and bees buzzing up high.

Insects, insects, where could they be?
Insects, insects under the tree.
In the cocoon the caterpillar lies
Ready for its life to start and fly.

Insects, insects, where could they be?
Insects, insects under the tree.
Worms and slugs and slithery bugs
Crawling along *swish, swash, swosh.*

Insects, insects, where could they be?
Insects, insects under the tree.

Jessica Livingstone (10)
West Twyford Primary School, Park Royal

Summer And Winter

Summer
Summer, the time when you have fun
When the sun shines on you
When you play with your friends.

Summer, when you eat ice cream
When you drink cold juice
When you're trying to find some shade.

Winter
Winter, when you're making a snowman
When you're having snowball fights
When you play with your friends.

Winter, when you're wearing a coat, hat and scarf
When you're drinking hot tea
When you're trying to get warm.

Natalia Sieczkarek (10)
West Twyford Primary School, Park Royal

Nature In My Garden

I put my hand through the long grass and felt the tickling ants,
There is so much life under the grass,
Ants scurry to and fro, like they are under a lot of stress,
Birds chirp socially from dawn to dusk,
Fresh plants meet the surface,
A gentle breeze rolls along the grass, like a gentle rolling of a wave,
New grass meets my nose, playing with my nose,
And plants brighten up my life!

Manita Gujral (9)
West Twyford Primary School, Park Royal

Summertime

When summer comes
Flowers come out
Everyone comes outside
To play with their friends
On trees birds singing a song
Everyone eats cold food
Like cold drinks, yummy, cold ice cream
In summer we have fun and rest
But summer is best.

Maham Sajjad
West Twyford Primary School, Park Royal

Red

Red looks like blood.
It sounds like a quiet cat,
But smells like a goat,
Feeling like water,
It tastes like chocolate.
It reminds me of blood.

Summayyah Khan (8)
West Twyford Primary School, Park Royal

If I Could Fly

If I could fly
I would go,
Over the fence,
Through the arch,
Across the bridge,
Over the hedge,
Above the lake,
In the alley
And that is where I found
A small little town,
Soon I went home
And that led me . . .
Up the alley,
Above the lake,
Over the hedge,
Across the bridge,
Through the arch
And all the way home.

Anjali Karadia (10)
West Twyford Primary School, Park Royal

Insects

Every insect
Is divided into three,
One head, one chest, one stomach part.
Some have brains,
All have a heart.
Insects have no bones,
No noses,
But with feelers they can smell
Dinner half a mile away.
Can your nose do half as well?
Also you'd be in fix
With all those legs to manage: six.

Rut Patel (10)
West Twyford Primary School, Park Royal

Happiness

I can see a sunny day
Hear birds tweeting
I can smell delicious melting chocolate
I'm on a beach
Tasting lots of ice cream
I wish I had all the toys in the world.

Robert Graham (9)
West Twyford Primary School, Park Royal

Friends!

Gazing at the bright blue sky,
Looking at the trees swaying from side to side.
As the colourful flowers laying in the grass shy
And all the children play with their bikes and say to their friends,
Would you like a ride?
I would pay anything to have a friend that can care for me
And always stay by my side wherever I go,
So she can sit with me and gaze at the sky.

Mennat Soliman (10)
West Twyford Primary School, Park Royal

Angry

I can see darkness of holes terrifying
I can hear the thunderstorm growling in the sky
Feeling your shots hitting sharply
I taste lots of fear like drinking red paint
The smell is like raw chicken, an odour creeping into my nose.
Anger reminds me of a dead rabbit.

Daniel Doroodvash (9)
West Twyford Primary School, Park Royal

A Friend To Me

You're a friend, a friend to me
You brighten up my day
You make the sun shine just like yesterday
When I laugh you laugh with me.
When in need you help indeed
You can be teased and be teased back.
A friend one day and not the next
But you're the best
You're a friend, a friend to me.

Tania Rull (10)
West Twyford Primary School, Park Royal

Playing

P laying is fun
L ying in the sun is cool
A s you run
Y ou sweat in the sun
I n midday light
N ow it is bright
G o swimming.

Zed Asassa (10)
West Twyford Primary School, Park Royal

Steven Gerrard

Football player
Liverpool captain
Brilliant goalscorer
Good midfielder
Liverpool supporter
Extraordinary shooter
Brave person
Injury beater
Best player.

Matthew Critchley (9)
Withnell Fold Primary School, Chorley

Brothers!

Annoying, greedy and loud,
When I'm trying to sleep they've friends round,
So I get most annoyed with their terrible sound,
No rest at all can be found.

They're greedy at my party,
And hog all the food,
When Mum leaves them in charge,
All they do is play pool.

They do make me glad,
When sometimes I'm sad,
And help when I fall,
Or when I am lonely.

On holiday they really care,
And are helpful, kind and good company,
But other times they are not fair,
I am really glad that they are both there,
But it would be good to have a sister to share.

Lucy Turnock (10)
Withnell Fold Primary School, Chorley

My Bedroom

My bedroom is a tip,
It looks like a skip,
I wish it was clean,
And then it would gleam.

Everything is everywhere,
To be honest, I really don't care.
My mum says to me, 'Tidy it up!'
I just tell her to *shut up!*

My mum and dad are mad at me,
But maybe they'll forget after tea!
My room is the messiest of all,
Even messier than our family hall!

Fionach Miller (10)
Withnell Fold Primary School, Chorley

Cat Memories

JJ, Jimmy, Jack and Ginny.
Cats I won't forget.

Jack is cool, funky and can really run,
Getting stuck in the loft to him was fun,
A long miaow, a hiss and a squeal,
A big pair of evil eyes so real.
His nickname is Flufter because he's so hairy,
To other cats he is quite scary.
I last saw him on the drive and gave him a glance,
When I was in the taxi going to France.

Ginny is like a second best friend,
Ninety-two in cat years and thirteen in ours.
She curls up on my bed for hours and hours,
She purrs like a cat movie star,
Never going out too far.

Jimmy is different,
One white paw but he is mainly black,
He's nicknamed 'Dogcat' because he lies on his back.
We lost him one day,
We put posters up around.
But he never came back I am sorry to say,
I hope he is alive, oh, I do, I do, I do.

JJ is lazy, cute and soft,
We thought he was going but luckily he came back.

I love all my cats
And I always will.

Megan Davis (10)
Withnell Fold Primary School, Chorley

A Horrible Spot On My Nose

When I looked in the mirror
On the tip of my nose,
What was it? I thought,
It was yellow and brown
With one hair on its end.
I looked harder and harder
I was sure it was a spot
A giant volcano that was about to *pop!*

Today I went shopping
With a mask on my face,
I felt so embarrassed
Oh what should I say?
Many people were laughing, smirking and whispering,
So I took off my mask
To reveal the thing.

Two days have passed
I knew the spot had grown fatter,
I felt so grumpy
So my mum asked me
'What is the matter?'
I tried squeezing it hard
But that didn't work.
What should I do?
As I walked out the door
I felt something erupting,
And the giant volcano
Went *pop! Pop! Pop!*

Kate Widdowson (11)
Withnell Fold Primary School, Chorley

My Family

James, my brother is very annoying,
He always hogs the TV.
When I'm away,
He goes into my room,
And takes some of my things I'm sad to say.

But he can be kind,
And he still cares for me,
And helps me with my homework.

My mum is also helpful,
Doing nearly all the housework,
Cooking, cleaning and washing,
I can tell her all my worries,
Even though she gets cross,
She's still the best mum ever.

Dad is friendly and funny,
He tells me lots of jokes,
Caring for us all and helping round the house,
Making me laugh when I'm upset,
He's really into sport.

I love all my family.

Anna Hopkin (10)
Withnell Fold Primary School, Chorley

Blue

Blue skies, blue seas, blue ink, blue eyes,
There are many different kinds of blue.
Neon turquoise, denim and navy,
All the colours you need.
A book, a pen, a crayon
And all the seasons in the year.
The blues, the jazz, the music, all have blue in them.
Movies like 'Jaws' have blue seas,
Green, yellow and red are all decent colours
But blue is the best, out of all the rest.

Thomas Radziminski (9)
Withnell Fold Primary School, Chorley

Ralph The Snake

Ralph is a wonderful scaly snake.
He is eight foot longer than a rake.
Ralph is a Californian king snake,
Excellent at swimming in a lake.
Ralph can twist himself into a knot,
Sometimes his prey can stink and rot.
Ralph likes dark places like down my jumper,
It makes me embarrassed because I look plumper.
Ralph strikes fast when he eats his food,
His manners aren't good, making him rude.
His eyes look grey when he sheds his skin,
And also he is as stinky as a bin.
He slithers round all day in his tank,
Even though this smells really rank.
He is the best snake in the world,
Today you can't replace him
With any amount of pay.

Rocky Widdowson (9)
Withnell Fold Primary School, Chorley

Ghost Ship

Jet-black sails in the dark night sky,
Skull and crossbones makes villagers cry.
'Oh no, it's the ghost ship, hide, all of you
Or the ghost ship will come and kidnap you too.'

Sailing through the mist like a knife slicing water,
The boat is Mexican from where the ghosts found her.
The ship sails on over huge tidal waves,
To come and make villagers the ghost pirates' slaves.

Inside their minds the ghost pirates hold,
Mysterious stories never to be told.
Good or bad, evil or kind,
Whatever the weather, the ghost pirates find . . .
Gold!

Harriet Tallon (11)
Withnell Fold Primary School, Chorley

My Dreams

In my dreams,
I can go anywhere,
Running in the park,
Or flying through the air.

Go to the sun,
On a holiday,
But no family allowed,
I'm sorry to say.

Go to my friends,
She lives far away.
That's a thought
I'll go today.

Blast off!
I'll go to the moon,
Through planets and stars,
I think I'll go soon.

Win a hundred pounds,
Now that's a good thought,
All for myself,
Don't be greedy, I was taught.

Can't wait for tonight,
So long it seems
Until I get back
To all my *dreams!*

Ali Wrigley (11)
Withnell Fold Primary School, Chorley

The Four Seasons

Why Winter, are you so cold?
So dark, so gloomy,
So wet, so damp,
I like it when you snow,
But otherwise you're so boring,
Why Winter, why?

Spring, how are you so beautiful?
So bright, so warm,
So much fun, so fine.
I don't like it when you sometimes rain,
But otherwise you're so warm,
How Spring, how?

Summer, when are you coming?
So long, so little to give.
So hot, so few clouds.
I hate it when you go and I'm waiting for your return,
But while you're here I love you.
When Summer, when?

Autumn, why are you making all the plants die back?
So much dying, so little plant life.
So much wishing to turn back time, so little plant life.
I like trailing through the fallen leaves,
But otherwise I don't like you turning cold again.
Why Autumn, why?

Joshua Jackson (11)
Withnell Fold Primary School, Chorley

Purple

My favourite colour is purple,
Can you think of anything purple?
I can!
I have thought of:
Grapes,
Sweets,
Materials,
My special mugs,
Cadbury's chocolate wrapper,
My ruler,
Paper or card,
Some bobbles,
Irises,
Covers on my bed,
My bedroom wall,
My rubber at school,
My fancy T-shirt,
My favourite felt-tip pen,
My best gel pen,
My friend's pencil case,
A book cover,
Violets.
Can you think of anything else purple?

Carla Davy (11)
Withnell Fold Primary School, Chorley

Friendship

Friends are great,
We call them mates.
Accommodating us all the way,
Making us laugh every day.
Every Saturday after sports, even when losing,
We are still good friends,
So we ask our mums, 'Can we play?'
Friends are trustworthy, helpful and kind,
You ask them to keep a secret,
'Do you not mind?'

We share with them our emotions,
They cheer us up,
Pat us on the back and say
'Will you be OK?'
I stand up feeling better,
The next day they send me a letter.

We have had bad days,
But those days are gone.
Friends are the best,
And are a huge, tremendous help.

Greg Smith (10)
Withnell Fold Primary School, Chorley

My Family

My brother is noisy
But he smiles all the time.
He helps me when I'm stuck,
He can be annoying sometimes,
But I still love him.

My baby sister is cute.
She now makes lots of sounds.
She is cheeky when she has her food,
She sticks her tongue out
Then cries when she needs her bottle,
But I still love her.

My mum looks after me when I'm ill.
She loves us all.
She helps me with my homework.
She also makes our tea.
She can be cross with us,
But I still love her.

My dad loves us very much.
But during the week, we don't see him very much.
He works very hard.

I love my family very much.

Sophie Parry (10)
Withnell Fold Primary School, Chorley

Hairdressers

Mama please don't do it
Don't make me go to the hairdressers
You know I love my hair, it's the best in the world
That the man will never, never chop
Because I will never get rid of it you know.

Mama please don't do it
Please don't take me to the hairdressers
You know I love my hair
Because my hair is so cool
You know I hate the hairdressers
When my hairs go down my shirt.

Mama please, please, please don't do it
We are at the hairdressers but don't do it
Ah! Oh no, you've chopped my beautiful hair
No! Actually it looks good, thanks Mum.

Lewis Gabbott (10)
Withnell Fold Primary School, Chorley

Brilliant Footballer

A Manchester United player
Also for England
Ambassador of the game
Young player of the year
Pushes players out of the way
Red and yellow cards too many to count
Determined to win
Champion centre forward
Always got money in his pocket
King of the volleys
Irreplaceable shooter
Speaks his mind
Who am I praising?
There can only be one
Wayne Rooney!

Daniel Lane (11)
Withnell Fold Primary School, Chorley

The Fierce Dragon

The gigantic dragon plodding along
Stomp! Stomp! Stomp!

His big strong body dragging him along,
Stomp! Stomp! Stomp!

His hot and fiery steaming breath,
Stomp! Stomp! Stomp!

His long barbed tail trailing behind,
Stomp! Stomp! Stomp!

In fact he's St George's enemy,
Stomp! Stomp! Stomp!

Oh my goodness!
The ugly beast is here!
I'm off!

Luke McCarrick (10)
Withnell Fold Primary School, Chorley

Spike

Spike is so cute
He's not a fright at night.
Beautiful coloured
Just like his mother.
He loves to walk and to talk.
He is a beautiful
Dog
A Jack Russell the sort
He may be small but he acts tall
When I am sad the lad cheers me
Up with a woof
He makes me smile, it's
Always worthwhile
He is a great dog to have.
He is never bad
That is why he is the
Top dog.

Natasha McMahon (11)
Withnell Fold Primary School, Chorley

My Grandad

My grandad used to read me stories
Play with me and take me to bed.
I always remember my dear old grandad
As he always made me laugh.

I have my grandfather's clock
It ticks and tocks when I am in bed.
I remember how he played statues
He often used his walking stick.

Turning round I always moved
What a great grandad I had.
My grandad had always loved me
Ever since I was a baby.

Tickling me, he made me laugh.
Now he has gone I really miss him.
I always remember the good times
I had with my grandad.

Bethany Wood (11)
Withnell Fold Primary School, Chorley

Good And Evil

Good is sharing
Good is caring.

Evil is destruction
Evil is war
It flows through the world like a plague.

Good is white
Evil is black
Good can bring happiness at the speed of light.

Evil is bullying
Evil is death
Evil is sadness
Evil is anger.

Good is risking your life for one another
In order to stop evil.

I hope the world will come to peace
And everybody will live in happiness.

Sam Fenton (9)
Withnell Fold Primary School, Chorley

Miffy

One great friend I had,
Miffy my rabbit.
She was never bad,
But never good,
Just in-between,
The way I like it!

She sat, lay, slept and played,
In her warm, soft cage in our garden.
Suddenly from behind the shed,
Popped out rats!
Smelly rats they were,
Trying to get my friend.

We couldn't keep her,
So I gave her to my good old friend Anna.
A few years later, Miffy started to get ill!
I got one last hold of my friend and said
Goodbye/
She was my best friend
    My Miffy!

Alice Sofield (9)
Withnell Fold Primary School, Chorley

My Best Friend, Cute But Bossy

Protective and loveable, a miniature schnauzer.
Annoyed easily
But I'm OK with that.
I love my dog.

All other dogs she barks at
Jealous of others being stroked.
She's Joss from Pontefract
And is a real boss.
I love my dog.

When I'm down she's a comfort
And makes me feel better
She likes going for walks
Anywhere we take her.
I love my dog.

Seeing her cute face
Was the best thing that ever happened to me.
She's now all grown up
And she is my best friend.
I love my dog
I love her very much.

Sam Cartwright (10)
Withnell Fold Primary School, Chorley